THE COMPLETE VEGETARIAN AIR FRYER COOKBOOK NEW EDITION

Over 1000+ Wholesome and Easy Air Fryer Recipes for Vegetarians—Quick, Tasty, and Healthy Meals for a Guilt-Free Lifestyle

NANCY A. BECKER

Copyright © 2024 By N A N C Y A . B E C K E R . All rights reserved worldwide.

No part of this book may be reproduced or transmitted in any form or by any means, electronic or mechanical, including photocopying, recording, or by any information storage and retrieval system, without written permission from the publisher, except for including brief quotations in a review.

Warning Disclaimer:

The purpose of this book is to educate and entertain. The author or publisher does not guarantee that anyone following the techniques, suggestions, tips, ideas, or strategies will become successful. The author and publisher shall have neither liability nor responsibility to anyone concerning any loss or damage caused, or alleged to be caused, directly or indirectly, by the information contained in this book.

This copyright notice and disclaimer apply to the entirety of the book and its contents, whether in print or electronic form and extend to all future editions or revisions of the book. Unauthorised use or reproduction of this book or its contents is strictly prohibited and may result in legal action.

TABLE OF CONTENTS

INTRODUCTION 7

   The Basics of Air Frying............9

   Air Fryer Safety and Maintenance 13

   Troubleshooting Common Issues 15

   Meal Planning and Prep............ 17

CHAPTER 1: BREAKFAST & BRUNCH 21

   Crispy Hash Brown Nests with Avocado 21

   Breakfast Burrito RollUps 21

   French Toast Sticks.................22

   Granola Clusters 23

   Stuffed Breakfast Peppers 23

   Crispy Tofu Scramble 24

   Sweet Potato Toast Two Ways 25

   Cinnamon Roll Bites 25

   Breakfast Quesadillas..............26

   Potato and Spinach Frittata.....27

   Apple Cinnamon Oatmeal Cups 27

   Cornmeal Pancake Bites..........28

   Breakfast Pizza Squares..........28

CHAPTER 2: SNACKS & APPETIZERS 29

   Crispy Cauliflower Wings..........29

   Stuffed Jalapeño Poppers 29

   Crispy Chickpeas Three Ways .30

   Vegetable Spring Rolls............. 31

   Mozzarella Sticks 31

   Crispy Mushroom "Calamari"...32

   Sweet Potato Crisps.................32

   Onion Bhajis 33

   Zucchini Chips.........................33

Spinach and Artichoke Rolls... 34

Corn Riblets 34

Buffalo Cauliflower Bites 35

Crispy Okra Fries 36

CHAPTER 3: VEGETABLES MADE EASY 37

Perfect Roasted Broccoli 37

Crispy Brussels Sprouts 37

Cauliflower Steaks 38

Stuffed Portobello Mushrooms 38

Sesame Green Beans 39

HoneyGlazed Carrots 39

Crispy Kale Chips 40

Corn on the Cob 40

Garlic Parmesan Asparagus 41

Mediterranean Aubergine Rounds 41

Crispy Courgette Fries 42

Sweet and Spicy Butternut Squash 43

HerbRoasted Root Vegetables 44

CHAPTER 4: MAIN DISHES 45

Crispy Tofu Katsu Curry 45

Stuffed Bell Peppers 46

Eggplant Parmesan 47

Cauliflower Steak Burger 48

Quinoa and Black Bean Patties 48

Mediterranean Stuffed Courgettes 49

Crispy Tempeh Buddha Bowl ... 50

Vegetable Lasagna RollUps 50

Tofu Fish and Chips 51

Stuffed Potato Skins 52

Chickpea and Spinach Patties .53

Mushroom Wellington 53

Lentil and Vegetable Loaf 54

CHAPTER 5: GLOBAL FLAVOURS ... 55

Indian Samosas 55

Mexican Bean and Cheese Taquitos 55

Italian Arancini Balls 56

Greek Spanakopita 57

Japanese Tempura Vegetables 57

Thai Spring Rolls 58

Middle Eastern Falafel 58

Chinese Salt and Pepper Tofu ..59

Vietnamese Banh Mi Rolls 59

Korean Kimchi Pancakes 60

Ethiopian Lentil Sambusas 60

Russian Potato Vareniki 61

Lebanese Spinach Fatayer 62

CHAPTER 6: KID-FRIENDLY FAVOURITES 64

Veggie Nuggets 63

Mac and Cheese Bites 63

Pizza Rolls 64

Sweet Potato Fries 64

Crispy Cucumber Coins............65

Cheesy Broccoli Tots 65

Rainbow Vegetable Skewers ...66

Corn Dogs................................66

Alphabet Potato Shapes...........67

VeggieLoaded Tater Tots 67

Crispy Avocado Fries 68

Hidden Vegetable Pasta Bake ..69

Fruit and Oat Cookies...............70

CHAPTER 7: PARTY FOOD & SHARING PLATES 71

Party Mix Snack Medley 71

Loaded Nachos 71

Buffalo Cauliflower Sliders 72

Crispy Wontons.......................73

Vegetable Antipasto Platter.....73

SevenLayer Dip Cups 74

Mini Calzones 74

Stuffed Mushroom Caps...........75

- Crispy Bruschetta Bites 75
- Vegetable Spring Roll Platter ... 76
- Cheese and Herb Breadsticks .. 76
- Party Pinwheels 77
- Sweet Potato Toast Canapés ... 78

CHAPTER 8: SIDES & ACCOMPANIMENTS 79

- Garlic Herb Roasted Potatoes .. 79
- Crispy Polenta Chips 79
- Mediterranean Roasted Vegetables 80
- Cauliflower Rice 80
- Crispy Quinoa 81
- Stuffed Baby Potatoes 81
- Herbed Dinner Rolls 82
- Crispy Onion Strings 82
- Roasted Cherry Tomatoes 83
- Green Bean Almondine 83
- Crispy Roasted Chickpeas 84
- Parmesan Zucchini Rounds 85
- Sweet Potato Wedges 86

CHAPTER 9: SAUCES & DIPS 87

- Roasted Red Pepper Hummus .. 87
- Spinach and Artichoke Dip 87
- Baked Ricotta 88
- Roasted Garlic Aioli 89
- Crispy Seasoned Oil 89
- Romesco Sauce 90
- Roasted Tomato Salsa 90
- Baba Ganoush 91
- Cashew Cheese Sauce 91
- Crispy Chickpea Hummus 92
- Roasted Vegetable Pesto 92
- Sweet Chili Sauce 93
- Smoky Vegan Queso 94

CHAPTER 10: DESSERTS 95

- Apple Crisps 95
- Cinnamon Sugar Churros 95

- Chocolate Lava Cakes 96
- Banana Fritters 97
- Berry Turnovers.......................97
- Crispy Peanut Butter Cups.......98
- Fruit Crumble 98
- Sweet Potato Brownies............99
- Crispy Pie Crust Cookies..........99
- Stuffed Baked Apples 100
- Chocolate Chip Cookie Cups .. 100
- Crispy Rice Pudding Balls 101
- Mini Fruit Pies 101

MEAL PLANNING AND NUTRITION GUIDE 102

- 60-day Meal Plan..................... 102
- Conversions and Substitutions 111

INTRODUCTION

MY JOURNEY TO VEGETARIAN AIR FRYER COOKING

I remember the day my air fryer first arrived like it was yesterday. There it sat, a rather imposing box on my kitchen worktop, promising crispy, guilt-free cooking—but I'll be honest, I was properly sceptical. As a lifelong vegetarian and someone who'd grown tired of soggy vegetables and bland meat alternatives, I couldn't help but wonder: could this gadget transform my cooking?

I'd always been passionate about vegetarian cooking, having grown up in a family where Sunday roasts meant nut loaves and Christmas dinner centred around a magnificent vegetable pie. But after years of relying on my trusty oven and hob, I found myself in a bit of a cooking rut. My partner had begun calling my goto recipes "the usual suspects," and even I had to admit that things had gotten boring.

That first evening, I decided to start simple—just some chunky chips made from local Maris Pipers. When I pulled out that basket 15 minutes later, I was gobsmacked. They were perfect: crispy on the outside, fluffy on the inside, and I'd used just a fraction of the oil I normally would. From that moment, I was hooked.

Over the next few months, I experimented with everything: crispy tofu that turned out crispy, homemade falafels that could rival my local takeaway and vegetables that my veg-dodging nephew now requests by name. There were some proper disasters along the way, mind—we don't talk about the Great Cauliflower Wing Incident of 2022—but each mishap taught me something new.

HOW THIS BOOK WILL TRANSFORM YOUR COOKING

Now, let me be clear: this isn't just another cookbook that'll end up gathering dust on your shelf. Whether you're a complete novice who's just unboxed your air fryer or someone looking to expand your veggie repertoire, I've written this book to be your kitchen companion, your cooking confidant, if you will.

Throughout these pages, you'll find:

Foolproof Techniques: I'll walk you through every step, from choosing the right air fryer to mastering temperature control. No more guesswork!

TimeSaving Tips: Because I know you've got better things to do than spend hours in the kitchen.

Ingredient Guides: We'll explore everything from different types of tofu to which vegetables create magic in your air fryer.

Troubleshooting Help: Those mistakes I mentioned? I've included solutions for every common air frying hiccup.

But more than just recipes, this book is about building confidence. Each chapter builds upon the last, gradually introducing new techniques and flavours. By the time you've cooked your way through, you'll be creating your air fryer masterpieces without so much as a glance at a recipe.

I've also included plenty of "Choose Your Own Adventure" options within recipes. Feeding picky eaters? Got a random vegetable that needs to be used up? Trying to up your protein intake? I've got you covered with substitutions and variations galore.

THE JOY AND BENEFITS OF VEGETARIAN AIR FRYING

Let's have a proper chat about why vegetarian air frying is such a game-changer, shall we? First off, it's an absolute blessing for anyone looking to make healthier choices without sacrificing flavour. By using just a tiny amount of oil—sometimes none at all—you can achieve that satisfying crispiness that usually comes from deep frying.

But the benefits go well beyond health:
Speed: Most recipes in this book take less than 30 minutes. Fancy a curry in a hurry? Sorted.
Energy Efficiency: Your air fryer uses far less electricity than heating a full-size oven.
Versatility: From breakfast to pudding, your air fryer can do it all.
Consistent Results: Once you've got your timings down, you'll get perfect results every time.

For us vegetarians, the air fryer is particularly brilliant because it solves so many common cooking challenges. No more mushy vegetables, soggy tofu, or burnt meat alternatives. Instead, you'll get perfectly cooked veggies with caramelised edges, tofu that's crispy on the outside and tender inside, and meat alternatives that could fool even the most dedicated carnivore.

And let's talk about the joy of it all. There's something properly satisfying about pulling out a basket of perfectly crispy buffalo cauliflower wings or watching your kids devour air-fried broccoli (yes, really!). It brings back the excitement of cooking, the willingness to experiment, and the pure pleasure of creating something delicious with your own hands.

As we embark on this air-frying adventure together, remember: this is meant to be fun. Yes, you'll learn loads, and yes, your cooking will transform, but at its heart, this book is about enjoying good food with the people you love. So, pop the kettle on, get comfortable, and let's get cooking!

THE BASICS OF AIR FRYING

WHAT IS AN AIR FRYER? AND HOW AIR FRYERS WORK

Let's demystify these clever little machines, shall we? Picture this: you're after that perfect chip—crispy on the outside, fluffy on the inside—but without drowning it in oil. That's where your air fryer comes in, working its magic through the simple science of hot air circulation.

Think of an air fryer as a miniature fan oven on steroids. At the top, you'll find a heating element and a powerful fan. When you pop your food in the basket and turn it on, the fan whizzes hot air around at top speed, creating a tornado of heat that circulates all around your food. This rapid air movement is what creates that lovely crispy exterior we're all after.

The real genius lies in how it uses this hot air. As it circulates, it creates an effect similar to deep frying, but—and here's the brilliant bit—it needs only a fraction of the oil. Sometimes, just a quick spritz will do! The hot air rapidly heats the outside of your food, creating that crispy layer we all love, while the inside stays perfectly cooked and moist.

TYPES OF AIR FRYERS

Now, when it comes to choosing an air fryer, you've got a few different types to consider:

1. BasketStyle Air Fryers
The most common type
Perfect for 12 people
Ideal for chips, vegetables, and smaller items
Usually the most affordable option
Takes up less counter space

2. OvenStyle Air Fryers
Larger capacity
Multiple cooking levels
Often comes with a rotisserie function
Great for families or batch-cooking
Can replace several kitchen appliances

3. Multifunction Cookers with Air Fry Feature
Combines multiple cooking methods
Good if you're short on space
Might not be as effective as dedicated air fryers
Often more expensive

CHOOSING THE RIGHT AIR FRYER FOR YOU

Right, let's get down to brass tacks. Choosing the perfect air fryer doesn't have to be a headache. Here's what I consider essential:

1. SIZE MATTERS
For singles or couples: 1.8-2.5 litres
Family of four: 3-5.5 litres
Larger families or batch cooking: 5.5+ litres

2. POWER
Look for 1400-1700 watts for optimal performance
More power generally means faster cooking

3. FEATURES TO CONSIDER
Digital vs dial controls (I prefer digital for precision)
Dishwasher-safe parts (trust me, this is a godsend)
Preset programs (brilliant for beginners)
Temperature range (wider is better)

4. BUDGET
Budget options: £30-£60
Midrange: £60-£100
Premium: £100+

Remember, the best air fryer is the one you'll use. In my experience, simple is often better—you don't need all the bells and whistles to make cracking food.

ESSENTIAL AIR FRYER ACCESSORIES

Now, while your air fryer will come with the basics, there are a few extras that I've found invaluable:

1. Oil Sprayer (£5£10)
- Essential for even oil distribution
- Helps achieve that perfect crisp
- Much better than aerosol cooking sprays

2. Extra Baskets (£10£20)
- Brilliant for batch cooking
- Allows you to prep the next batch while one's cooking

3. Silicone Trivet (£5£15)
- Protects your worktop
- Doubles as a heat-safe place to put hot baskets

4. Parchment Liners (£5 for 100)
- Makes cleanup a doddle
- Perfect for sticky foods or battered items

5. HeatResistant Tongs (£5£10)
- For safely removing food
- Look for silicone-tipped ones to protect the basket's coating

AIR FRYER VS TRADITIONAL COOKING METHODS
HEALTH BENEFITS

Let's talk about the elephant in the room—is air frying healthier? In my experience, the answer is a resounding yes, and here's why:

1. Reduced Oil Usage
- Traditional frying: 3 tablespoons or more of oil
- Air frying: Often just 1 teaspoon or less
- Potential calorie reduction: 7080%

2. Retained Nutrients
- Shorter cooking times mean more nutrients stay in your veg
- No nutrient loss through the water as with boiling

3. Acrylamide Reduction
Air frying can reduce acrylamide (a potentially harmful compound) by up to 90% compared to deep frying
Particularly important for potato products

4. Better Portion Control
Basket size naturally limits portions
Less temptation to cook extra "while the oil's hot"

I've found that switching to air frying has made it much easier to stick to healthier cooking methods without feeling like I'm missing out on my favourite crispy treats.

TIME AND ENERGY EFFICIENCY

Time is precious, isn't it? Here's how air fryers can help you save both time and pennies:

1. Cooking Times
Traditional Oven vs Air Fryer:
Chips: 2530 mins vs 1518 mins
Roasted veg: 2025 mins vs 1012 mins
Frozen foods: 2025 mins vs 812 mins

2. Energy Usage
Average oven: 2.3 kWh per hour
Average air fryer: 1.5 kWh per hour
Potential energy saving: 3040%

3. Practical Benefits
No preheating is required (usually)
Easy cleanup (most parts are dishwasher safe)
Less kitchen heat in summer
Can often cook straight from frozen

A quick tip: I keep a cooking diary noting times and temperatures for different recipes. It's amazing how quickly you can build up a personalised cooking guide!

AIR FRYER SAFETY AND MAINTENANCE

SAFETY GUIDELINES

Let's start with the crucial bits—keeping you and your air fryer safe and sound. I know it might seem like common sense, but after teaching countless cooking classes, I've learned that a quick safety refresher never goes amiss.

ESSENTIAL SAFETY RULES

1. Placement Matters
Keep at least 10cm of space around all sides
Always use on a heat-resistant, level surface
Never put your air fryer against a wall or under cabinets

My Tip: I keep a silicone mat undermined—saves the worktop and stops it from sliding about!

2. Electrical Safety
Check the cord regularly for any damage
Never use an extension lead—plug directly into the socket
Keep away from water sources (sinks, etc.)
Unplug when not in use (saves a few pennies too!)

3. Fire Prevention
Never add oil to the bottom of the basket
Clean after each use to prevent grease buildup
Don't overfill—food needs room to circulate!

Crisis Control: If you spot smoke, don't panic! Unplug immediately and keep the basket closed until it stops.

4. Avoiding Burns
Use oven gloves or tongs to handle hot parts
Be mindful of steam when opening the basket
Keep children and pets away during use
Allow to cool completely before moving or cleaning

Special Considerations for Vegetarian Cooking

Light ingredients (like leafy greens) can fly about—use a trivet or rack to keep them in place.
Some meat alternatives can release a lot of liquid—check halfway through cooking.
Marinated tofu or seitan can drip—place a piece of foil in the bottom basket to catch drips.

CLEANING AND MAINTENANCE TIPS

Keeping your air fryer spick and span isn't just about appearances—it's essential for both safety and performance. Here's my tested cleaning routine:

AFTER EACH USE

1. Unplug and let cool completely

2. Remove and clean the basket and pan
Warm, soapy water works best
Use a non-abrasive sponge
Most are dishwasher safe, but hand washing extends their life

3. Wipe the interior with a damp cloth

WEEKLY DEEP CLEAN

1. Clean the heating element
Turn upside down and wipe with a damp cloth
Use a soft brush to remove any stuck bits

2. Clean the exterior
A damp cloth with mild detergent
Pay special attention to air vents

3. Check for any loose parts or damage

My Secret Weapon: A mixture of bicarbonate of soda and water makes a brilliant paste for tackling stubborn, baked bits!

TROUBLESHOOTING COMMON ISSUES

Even the best air fryers can sometimes act up. Here's how to sort out common niggles:

1. Food Not Crispy Enough
Cause: Too much moisture or overcrowding
Fix:
  Pat food dry before cooking
  Cook in smaller batches
  Give food a quick spray of oil

2. Uneven Cooking
Cause: Food pieces of different sizes or overcrowding
Fix:
  Cut vegetables to similar sizes
  Shake the basket halfway through cooking
  Don't stack food too high

3. White Smoke Coming from Unit
Cause: Usually excess grease
Fix:
  Clean thoroughly between uses
  Add a splash of water to the bottom basket for fatty foods

4. The Unit Won't Turn On
Cause: Often safety switch issues
Fix:
  Check basket is fully inserted
  Ensure the plug is securely in the socket
  Check for tripped circuit breaker

TECHNIQUES AND TIPS

Temperature Guide

Getting the temperature right is key to air fryer success. Here's my goto guide:

Temperature | Best For | Examples
160°C (320°F) | Delicate vegetables | Asparagus, Green Beans
180°C (350°F) | Most vegetables | Cauliflower, Broccoli
200°C (390°F) | Crispy items | Chips, Crispy Tofu

Temperature Tips
Start lower than you think—you can always add time
For frozen foods, reduce the temp by 10°C and increase the time by 20%
When adapting regular recipes, reduce the temp by 20°C

TIMING GUIDELINES
Timing is everything! Here's a handy reference:
Food Item | Time | Top Tips

Fresh-cut chips | 15-18 mins | Soak in water first
Cauliflower florets | 10-12 mins | Toss in oil and seasoning
Tofu cubes | 12-15 mins | Press and marinate first
Breaded vegetables | 8-10 mins | Spray with oil for colour

Pro Tip: I always set the timer for slightly less than I think—you can add more time, but you can't uncrisp overdone veg!

Preheating
The great preheating debate! Here's my take:

When to Preheat
Yes for:
  Crispy items like chips
  Baked goods
  When adapting oven recipes

No for:
  Most vegetables
  Reheating leftovers
  When time is tight!

Preheating Guide
1. Add 3 minutes to your cooking time
2. Let the air fryer run empty
3. Add food as soon as it's heated

TimeSaving Tip: If not preheating, add 2-3 minutes to your cooking time

BATCH COOKING
Master batch cooking and you'll be an air fryer pro in no time!

BATCH COOKING STRATEGIES

1. Prep Ahead
   Cut all vegetables to similar sizes
   Have containers ready for cooked food
   Keep a notepad handy for timing

2. Temperature Tactics
   Start with foods needing lower temps
   Work your way up to hotter items
   Use the residual heat wisely

3. Clever Combos
   Cook similar items together
   Use dividers or foil to separate flavours
   Think about cooking times when combining

MY FAVOURITE BATCH COOKING MENU
1. Start: Roasted garlic (160°C, 15 mins)
2. Next: Mixed vegetables (180°C, 12 mins)
3. Finish: Crispy tofu (200°C, 15 mins)

While one batch cooks, prep the next—it's like a vegetarian air-frying dance!

Remember: Every air fryer is a bit different, so use these guidelines as a starting point and adjust to your specific model. Keep notes of what works best for you—you'll be an expert in no time!

MEAL PLANNING AND PREP

Weekly Meal Planning Guide
Let's get organised, shall we? As a busy vegetarian cook, I've found that a bit of planning goes a long way—especially when it comes to air fryer cooking.

GETTING STARTED WITH MEAL PLANNING

1. The Basic Framework
  Here's my tested weekly plan structure:
   23 "proper cooking" nights

2 quick and easy meals
1 "cook once, eat twice" meal
1 flexible night (leftovers or takeaway)
Top Tip: Start small! Plan just 34 days at first, then work up to a full week.

2. STRATEGIC PLANNING
Day | Meal Type | Why It Works
Monday | Quick & Easy | Ease into the week
Tuesday | Proper Cooking | More energy after Monday
Wednesday | Leftovers/Quick | Midweek simplicity
Thursday | Proper Cooking | Second wind!
Friday | Fun & Flexible | End of week treat
Saturday | Batch Cooking | More time available
Sunday | Cook Once, Eat Twice | Prep for Monday

STORAGE AND REHEATING GUIDELINES
Proper Storage
Let's keep your air fryer creations fresh and tasty:

1. REFRIGERATOR STORAGE
Food Type | Container | Max Storage Time
Cooked vegetables | Airtight container | 34 days
Crispy items | Paper towel lined container | 2 days
Sauces & dips | Glass jar | 5 days
Prepared raw veg | Produce saver container | 5 days

2. FREEZER STORAGE
Food Type | Packaging | Max Storage Time
Veggie burgers | Freezer bag with parchment | 3 months
Breaded items | Freezer safe container | 2 months
Cooked vegetables | Freezer bag | 6 months
Always cool completely before freezing!

REHEATING IN THE AIR FRYER

The air fryer isn't just brilliant for cooking—it's a game-changer for reheating too!

1. General Reheating Guidelines
Food Type | Temperature | Time | Tips
- Crispy items | 180°C | 34 mins | Spread in single layer
- Vegetables | 160°C | 23 mins | Spritz with water
- Veggie burgers | 170°C | 45 mins | Flip halfway

2. Reheating from Frozen
- No need to thaw most items
- Add 50% to the regular cooking time
- Check frequently to avoid overcooking

3. Bringing Back the Crunch
- For soggy items, start at a lower temp (160°C) then finish hot (200°C)
- Use the air fryer basket, not additional trays or pans
- Don't overcrowd—reheat in batches if needed

REVIVING SPECIFIC FOODS

Food Item | Method | Special Tips
- Chips | 200°C for 34 mins | Shake halfway
- Roasted veg | 180°C for 23 mins | Spritz with oil
- Breaded items | 180°C for 45 mins | Space well apart

TIMESAVING TIPS

1. Prep Day Essentials
- Wash and chop vegetables
- Make sauces and dips
- Prepare marinades
- Cook grains and legumes

2. Kitchen Command Centre
- Keep a magnetic notepad on your fridge
- Note what needs using up
- List meal ideas for the week
- Track successful recipes and timings

3. The 'Bottom of the Fridge' Rescue Meal
Got random veg to use up? Try my formula:
1. Chop everything to similar sizes
2. Toss with oil and seasonings
3. Air fry at 180°C for 10-12 minutes
4. Serve over grains or greens

I call this my "Fridge Forage Feast"—different every time!

Remember: Meal planning isn't about being rigid—it's about making your life easier and ensuring you always have something tasty to eat. Be flexible, and don't be too hard on yourself if plans change!

CHAPTER 1: BREAKFAST & BRUNCH

CRISPY HASH BROWN NESTS WITH AVOCADO

Prep: 10 mins | **Cook:** 15 mins | **Serves:** 4
Cooking Function: Air Fry
Ingredients:

UK: 500g potatoes (grated), 1 tablespoon olive oil, 1/2 teaspoon garlic powder, 1/2 teaspoon onion powder, salt, pepper, 2 ripe avocados (sliced)

US: 1 lb potatoes (grated), 1 tablespoon olive oil, 1/2 teaspoon garlic powder, 1/2 teaspoon onion powder, salt, pepper, 2 ripe avocados (sliced)

Instructions:
1. Preheat your air fryer to 180°C (350°F).
2. In a bowl, mix the grated potatoes with olive oil, garlic powder, onion powder, salt, and pepper.
3. Scoop the potato mixture into a greased muffin tin, pressing it down to create little nests.
4. Place the muffin tin in the air fryer and cook for 1215 minutes, or until the hash browns are crispy and golden.
5. Remove the nests and let them cool for a few minutes before popping them out.
6. Top each nest with avocado slices and sprinkle with a little extra salt and pepper.
7. Serve warm and enjoy a crispy, flavour-packed breakfast.

Nutritional Info: Calories: 230 | Fat: 15g | Carbs: 20g | Protein: 2g

BREAKFAST BURRITO ROLLUPS

Prep: 10 mins | **Cook:** 10 mins | **Serves:** 4
Cooking Function: Air Fry
Ingredients:

UK: 4 medium flour tortillas, 200g scrambled tofu, 50g red bell pepper (diced), 50g red onion (diced), 100g cheddar cheese (grated), 1 tablespoon olive oil, salt, pepper

US: 4 medium flour tortillas, 7 oz scrambled tofu, 2 oz red bell pepper (diced), 2 oz red onion (diced), 4 oz cheddar cheese (grated), 1 tablespoon olive oil, salt, pepper

Instructions:
1. Preheat your air fryer to 180°C (350°F).
2. Lay out the tortillas and divide the scrambled tofu, red bell pepper, red onion, and cheese evenly among them.
3. Roll each tortilla tightly, tucking in the sides as you go to make a burrito shape.
4. Brush each burrito lightly with olive oil and season with a pinch of salt and pepper.
5. Place the burritos in the air fryer basket, seam side down, and cook for 810 minutes until golden and crispy.
6. Serve hot with your favourite salsa or avocado on the side.

Nutritional Info: Calories: 280 | Fat: 12g | Carbs: 32g | Protein: 12g

FRENCH TOAST STICKS

Prep: 5 mins | **Cook:** 8 mins | **Serves:** 4

Cooking Function: Air Fry

Ingredients:

UK: 4 thick slices of bread (cut into sticks), 2 large eggs, 100ml milk, 1 teaspoon vanilla extract, 1 tablespoon sugar, 1 teaspoon cinnamon, maple syrup (for serving)

US: 4 thick slices of bread (cut into sticks), 2 large eggs, 1/3 cup milk, 1 teaspoon vanilla extract, 1 tablespoon sugar, 1 teaspoon cinnamon, maple syrup (for serving)

Instructions:
1. Preheat your air fryer to 180°C (350°F).
2. In a shallow dish, whisk together the eggs, milk, vanilla, sugar, and cinnamon.
3. Dip each breadstick into the egg mixture, making sure it's well coated.
4. Place the coated bread sticks in a single layer in the air fryer basket.
5. Cook for 68 minutes, flipping halfway through, until golden and crispy.
6. Serve with maple syrup for dipping and enjoy!

Nutritional Info: Calories: 250 | Fat: 9g | Carbs: 34g | Protein: 8g

GRANOLA CLUSTERS

Prep: 10 mins | **Cook:** 12 mins | **Serves:** 6
Cooking Function: Air Fry
Ingredients:

UK: 200g rolled oats, 50g chopped almonds, 50g sunflower seeds, 50ml maple syrup, 30ml coconut oil (melted), 1 teaspoon cinnamon, 1/2 teaspoon vanilla extract

US: 2 cups rolled oats, 1/4 cup chopped almonds, 1/4 cup sunflower seeds, 1/4 cup maple syrup, 2 tablespoons coconut oil (melted), 1 teaspoon cinnamon, 1/2 teaspoon vanilla extract

Instructions:

1. Preheat your air fryer to 160°C (320°F).
2. In a large bowl, combine the oats, almonds, sunflower seeds, cinnamon, and a pinch of salt.
3. Stir in the maple syrup, melted coconut oil, and vanilla extract until everything is well coated.
4. Scoop the mixture into the air fryer basket, pressing it down slightly to form clusters.
5. Air fry for 10-12 minutes, shaking halfway through until the granola is golden and crisp.
6. Let it cool before breaking it into chunks. Store in an airtight container and serve over yoghurt or with milk.

Nutritional Info: Calories: 220 | Fat: 11g | Carbs: 28g | Protein: 5g

STUFFED BREAKFAST PEPPERS

Prep: 10 mins | **Cook:** 12 mins | **Serves:** 4
Cooking Function: Air Fry
Ingredients:

UK: 4 bell peppers (halved and deseeded), 200g scrambled tofu, 50g spinach (chopped), 50g cherry tomatoes (halved), 50g feta cheese (crumbled), 1 tablespoon olive oil, salt, pepper

US: 4 bell peppers (halved and deseeded), 7 oz scrambled tofu, 2 oz spinach (chopped), 2 oz cherry tomatoes (halved), 2 oz feta cheese (crumbled), 1 tablespoon olive oil, salt, pepper

Instructions:
1. Preheat your air fryer to 180°C (350°F).
2. In a pan, sauté the spinach in olive oil until wilted, then mix it with the scrambled tofu and cherry tomatoes. Season with salt and pepper.
3. Stuff each pepper half with the tofu mixture and top with crumbled feta cheese.
4. Place the stuffed peppers in the air fryer basket and cook for 1012 minutes, until the peppers are tender and the cheese is golden.
5. Serve hot and enjoy a colourful, protein-packed breakfast.

Nutritional Info: Calories: 180 | Fat: 9g | Carbs: 12g | Protein: 9g

CRISPY TOFU SCRAMBLE

Prep: 10 mins | **Cook:** 12 mins | **Serves:** 4

Cooking Function: Air Fry

Ingredients:

UK: 300g firm tofu (pressed and crumbled), 1 tablespoon olive oil, 1/2 teaspoon turmeric, 1/2 teaspoon paprika, 1/2 teaspoon garlic powder, 50g spinach (chopped), 50g red bell pepper (diced), salt, pepper

US: 10 oz firm tofu (pressed and crumbled), 1 tablespoon olive oil, 1/2 teaspoon turmeric, 1/2 teaspoon paprika, 1/2 teaspoon garlic powder, 2 oz spinach (chopped), 2 oz red bell pepper (diced), salt, pepper

Instructions:
1. Preheat your air fryer to 180°C (350°F).
2. In a bowl, toss the crumbled tofu with olive oil, turmeric, paprika, garlic powder, salt, and pepper.
3. Add the chopped spinach and diced red bell pepper to the mixture and stir well.
4. Transfer the tofu mixture to the air fryer basket in an even layer.
5. Air fry for 1012 minutes, stirring halfway through until the tofu is crispy on the edges.
6. Serve hot with toast or as a filling for wraps.

Nutritional Info: Calories: 170 | Fat: 10g | Carbs: 6g | Protein: 15g

SWEET POTATO TOAST TWO WAYS

Prep: 5 mins | **Cook:** 10 mins | **Serves:** 4
Cooking Function: Air Fry

Ingredients:

UK: 2 medium sweet potatoes (sliced into 1cm thick rounds), 1 tablespoon olive oil, 1 ripe avocado (sliced), 2 tablespoons peanut butter, 1 tablespoon honey, 1/2 teaspoon cinnamon, salt, pepper

US: 2 medium sweet potatoes (sliced into 1/2-inch-thick rounds), 1 tablespoon olive oil, 1 ripe avocado (sliced), 2 tablespoons peanut butter, 1 tablespoon honey, 1/2 teaspoon cinnamon, salt, pepper

Instructions:

1. Preheat your air fryer to 200°C (390°F).
2. Lightly brush the sweet potato slices with olive oil and sprinkle with salt and pepper.
3. Air fry the sweet potato slices for 810 minutes, flipping halfway until they're golden and tender.
4. For the first topping, spread peanut butter on half of the sweet potato slices and drizzle with honey and a pinch of cinnamon.
5. For the second topping, layer the other half with sliced avocado and season with extra salt and pepper.
6. Serve immediately and enjoy the variety!

Nutritional Info: Calories: 230 | Fat: 12g | Carbs: 26g | Protein: 4g

CINNAMON ROLL BITES

Prep: 5 mins | **Cook:** 10 mins | **Serves:** 4
Cooking Function: Air Fry

Ingredients:

UK: 1 can of readymade puff pastry (sliced into bitesize pieces), 50g butter (melted), 50g sugar, 1 tablespoon cinnamon, 100g icing sugar, 1 tablespoon milk

US: 1 can of readymade puff pastry (sliced into bitesize pieces), 4 tablespoons butter (melted), 1/4 cup sugar, 1 tablespoon cinnamon, 1/2 cup powdered sugar, 1 tablespoon milk

Instructions:
1. Preheat your air fryer to 180°C (350°F).
2. In a small bowl, mix the sugar and cinnamon.
3. Dip each puff pastry piece in melted butter, then coat in the cinnamon sugar mixture.
4. Place the pieces in a single layer in the air fryer basket and cook for 8-10 minutes, until golden and crispy.
5. While they cook, whisk together the icing sugar and milk to make a simple glaze.
6. Drizzle the cinnamon roll bites with glaze and serve warm for a sweet treat.

Nutritional Info: Calories: 300 | Fat: 18g | Carbs: 35g | Protein: 2g

BREAKFAST QUESADILLAS

Prep: 10 mins | **Cook:** 10 mins | **Serves:** 4
Cooking Function: Air Fry

Ingredients:
UK: 4 medium flour tortillas, 200g scrambled tofu, 100g cheddar cheese (grated), 50g black beans (drained and rinsed), 1 tablespoon olive oil, salsa (for serving)

US: 4 medium flour tortillas, 7 oz scrambled tofu, 4 oz cheddar cheese (grated), 2 oz black beans (drained and rinsed), 1 tablespoon olive oil, salsa (for serving)

Instructions:
1. Preheat your air fryer to 180°C (350°F).
2. Divide the scrambled tofu, cheese, and black beans evenly among the tortillas, folding each one in half to create a quesadilla.
3. Brush each quesadilla lightly with olive oil on both sides.
4. Place the quesadillas in the air fryer basket and cook for 8-10 minutes, flipping halfway through, until golden and crispy.
5. Slice and serve with salsa on the side for dipping.

Nutritional Info: Calories: 290 | Fat: 13g | Carbs: 32g | Protein: 13g

POTATO AND SPINACH FRITTATA

Prep: 10 mins | **Cook:** 15 mins | **Serves:** 4
Cooking Function: Air Fry
Ingredients:

UK: 300g potatoes (thinly sliced), 100g spinach (chopped), 6 large eggs, 50g feta cheese (crumbled), 1 tablespoon olive oil, salt, pepper

US: 10 oz potatoes (thinly sliced), 4 oz spinach (chopped), 6 large eggs, 2 oz feta cheese (crumbled), 1 tablespoon olive oil, salt, pepper

Instructions:
1. Preheat your air fryer to 180°C (350°F).
2. In a large bowl, whisk the eggs and season with salt and pepper.
3. Toss the potato slices in olive oil and lay them in a greased air fryersafe dish.
4. Pour the eggs over the potatoes, then sprinkle the chopped spinach and feta cheese on top.
5. Air fry for 1215 minutes, or until the eggs are set and the frittata is golden on top.
6. Let it cool for a minute, slice, and serve.

Nutritional Info: Calories: 220 | Fat: 12g | Carbs: 15g | Protein: 11g

APPLE CINNAMON OATMEAL CUPS

Prep: 10 mins | **Cook:** 12 mins | **Serves:** 6
Cooking Function: Air Fry
Ingredients:

UK: 150g rolled oats, 50g apples (diced), 200ml almond milk, 1 tablespoon maple syrup, 1 teaspoon cinnamon, 1/2 teaspoon baking powder, 1 tablespoon chia seeds

US: 1 1/2 cups rolled oats, 1/4 cup apples (diced), 3/4 cup almond milk, 1 tablespoon maple syrup, 1 teaspoon cinnamon, 1/2 teaspoon baking powder, 1 tablespoon chia seeds

Instructions:
1. Preheat your air fryer to 180°C (350°F).
2. In a large bowl, combine the oats, diced apples, cinnamon, chia seeds, and baking powder.
3. Stir in the almond milk and maple syrup until the mixture is well combined.
4. Scoop the mixture into greased muffin cups, filling them about two-thirds full.
5. Air fry for 1012 minutes, or until the oatmeal cups are firm and lightly golden.
6. Let them cool for a few minutes before serving. Enjoy a grab-and-go breakfast!

Nutritional Info: Calories: 160 | Fat: 4g | Carbs: 25g | Protein: 4g

CORNMEAL PANCAKE BITES

Prep: 5 mins | **Cook:** 8 mins | **Serves:** 4
Cooking Function: Air Fry
Ingredients:
UK: 100g cornmeal, 100g flour, 1 tablespoon sugar, 1/2 teaspoon baking powder, 150ml milk, 1 large egg, 1 tablespoon butter (melted), maple syrup (for serving)
US: 1/2 cup cornmeal, 1/2 cup flour, 1 tablespoon sugar, 1/2 teaspoon baking powder, 1/2 cup milk, 1 large egg, 1 tablespoon butter (melted), maple syrup (for serving)
Instructions:
1. Preheat your air fryer to 180°C (350°F).
2. In a bowl, whisk together the cornmeal, flour, sugar, and baking powder.
3. Stir in the milk, egg, and melted butter until smooth.
4. Scoop small spoonfuls of the batter into greased silicone muffin cups.
5. Air fry for 68 minutes, or until golden and puffed up.
6. Serve with maple syrup for dipping.
Nutritional Info: Calories: 190 | Fat: 7g | Carbs: 28g | Protein: 4g

BREAKFAST PIZZA SQUARES

Prep: 10 mins | **Cook:** 12 mins | **Serves:** 4
Cooking Function: Air Fry
Ingredients:
UK: 1 readymade pizza dough, 3 large eggs (beaten), 50g cheddar cheese (grated), 50g cherry tomatoes (halved), 1 tablespoon olive oil, salt, pepper
US: 1 readymade pizza dough, 3 large eggs (beaten), 2 oz cheddar cheese (grated), 2 oz cherry tomatoes (halved), 1 tablespoon olive oil, salt, pepper
Instructions:
1. Preheat your air fryer to 180°C (350°F).
2. Roll out the pizza dough and cut it into 4 square pieces.
3. Place the dough squares in the air fryer basket and brush with olive oil.
4. Top each square with a bit of beaten egg, grated cheese, and cherry tomatoes.
5. Season with salt and pepper and air fry for 1012 minutes, or until the dough is golden and the eggs are set.
6. Serve immediately for a fun and tasty breakfast.
Nutritional Info: Calories: 250 | Fat: 12g | Carbs: 28g | Protein: 10g

CHAPTER 2: SNACKS & APPETIZERS

CRISPY CAULIFLOWER WINGS

Prep: 15 mins | **Cook:** 20 mins | **Serves:** 4
Cooking Function: Air Fry
Ingredients:

UK: 1 medium cauliflower (cut into florets), 120g plain flour, 240ml water, 1 teaspoon garlic powder, 1 teaspoon paprika, salt, pepper, 100ml hot sauce, 2 tablespoons butter (melted)

US: 1 medium cauliflower (cut into florets), 1 cup plain flour, 1 cup water, 1 teaspoon garlic powder, 1 teaspoon paprika, salt, pepper, ½ cup hot sauce, 2 tablespoons butter (melted)

Instructions:
1. Preheat your air fryer to 200°C (390°F).
2. In a bowl, whisk together flour, water, garlic powder, paprika, salt, and pepper until smooth.
3. Dip each cauliflower floret into the batter, shaking off excess, and place them in the air fryer basket.
4. Air fry for 15 minutes, turning halfway through, until golden and crispy.
5. Meanwhile, mix the hot sauce and melted butter in a separate bowl.
6. Toss the crispy cauliflower wings in the hot sauce mixture and return to the air fryer for an additional 5 minutes to set the sauce.
7. Serve immediately with your favourite dip.

Nutritional Info: Calories: 180 | Fat: 7g | Carbs: 24g | Protein: 5g

STUFFED JALAPEÑO POPPERS

Prep: 10 mins | **Cook:** 12 mins | **Serves:** 4
Cooking Function: Air Fry
Ingredients:

UK: 12 large jalapeños (halved and seeds removed), 150g cream cheese, 50g cheddar cheese (grated), 2 tablespoons chopped chives, 50g breadcrumbs, 1 tablespoon olive oil

US: 12 large jalapeños (halved and seeds removed), 5 oz cream cheese, 2 oz cheddar cheese (grated), 2 tablespoons chopped chives, ½ cup breadcrumbs, 1 tablespoon olive oil

Instructions:
1. Preheat your air fryer to 180°C (350°F).
2. In a bowl, mix cream cheese, cheddar, and chives.
3. Spoon the cheese mixture into each jalapeño half.
4. In another bowl, toss the breadcrumbs with olive oil.
5. Sprinkle the breadcrumbs over the stuffed jalapeños.
6. Air fry for 1012 minutes, or until the tops are golden and crispy.
7. Serve hot with a cool dip on the side.

Nutritional Info: Calories: 150 | Fat: 10g | Carbs: 10g | Protein: 4g

CRISPY CHICKPEAS THREE WAYS

Prep: 5 mins | **Cook:** 15 mins | **Serves:** 4

Cooking Function: Air Fry

Ingredients:

UK: 400g tin chickpeas (drained and rinsed), 1 tablespoon olive oil, salt, 1 teaspoon cumin, 1 teaspoon smoked paprika, 1 teaspoon garlic powder (or your choice of seasoning)

US: 15 oz tin chickpeas (drained and rinsed), 1 tablespoon olive oil, salt, 1 teaspoon cumin, 1 teaspoon smoked paprika, 1 teaspoon garlic powder (or your choice of seasoning)

Instructions:
1. Preheat your air fryer to 200°C (390°F).
2. Pat the chickpeas dry with kitchen paper, then toss them in olive oil and your preferred seasoning.
3. Spread the chickpeas in a single layer in the air fryer basket.
4. Air fry for 1215 minutes, shaking halfway through, until crispy.
5. Enjoy them as a snack or sprinkle over salads for added crunch.

Nutritional Info: Calories: 120 | Fat: 4g | Carbs: 17g | Protein: 5g

VEGETABLE SPRING ROLLS

Prep: 20 mins | Cook: 10 mins | Serves: 4
Cooking Function: Air Fry
Ingredients:

UK: 8 spring roll wrappers, 1 carrot (julienned), 50g cabbage (shredded), 50g bean sprouts, 2 tablespoons soy sauce, 1 tablespoon sesame oil, 1 tablespoon olive oil

US: 8 spring roll wrappers, 1 carrot (julienned), 2 oz cabbage (shredded), 2 oz bean sprouts, 2 tablespoons soy sauce, 1 tablespoon sesame oil, 1 tablespoon olive oil

Instructions:

1. Preheat your air fryer to 190°C (375°F).
2. In a pan, sauté the carrot, cabbage, and bean sprouts with soy sauce and sesame oil for 3-4 minutes until softened.
3. Spoon the vegetable mixture onto each spring roll wrapper and fold them up tightly.
4. Brush each spring roll with olive oil and place them in the air fryer basket.
5. Air fry for 8-10 minutes, turning halfway through, until golden and crisp.
6. Serve with soy sauce or sweet chilli dipping sauce.

Nutritional Info: Calories: 160 | Fat: 8g | Carbs: 20g | Protein: 3g

MOZZARELLA STICKS

Prep: 10 mins | Cook: 8 mins | Serves: 4
Cooking Function: Air Fry
Ingredients:

UK: 8 mozzarella sticks, 50g breadcrumbs, 2 eggs (beaten), 50g plain flour, 1 teaspoon dried oregano, salt, pepper

US: 8 mozzarella sticks, ½ cup breadcrumbs, 2 eggs (beaten), ½ cup plain flour, 1 teaspoon dried oregano, salt, pepper

Instructions:

1. Preheat your air fryer to 180°C (350°F).
2. Set up a breading station with three bowls: one with flour, one with beaten eggs, and one with breadcrumbs mixed with oregano, salt, and pepper.
3. Coat each mozzarella stick in flour, dip into the egg, and then coat in the breadcrumb mixture.
4. Place the mozzarella sticks in the air fryer and cook for 6-8 minutes, until crispy and golden.
5. Serve immediately with marinara sauce for dipping.

Nutritional Info: Calories: 220 | Fat: 12g | Carbs: 14g | Protein: 10g

CRISPY MUSHROOM "CALAMARI"

Prep: 10 mins | **Cook:** 10 mins | **Serves:** 4
Cooking Function: Air Fry

Ingredients:

UK: 300g oyster mushrooms (cut into strips), 50g breadcrumbs, 2 tablespoons plain flour, 1 teaspoon garlic powder, 1 teaspoon smoked paprika, 2 eggs (beaten), salt, pepper

US: 10 oz oyster mushrooms (cut into strips), ½ cup breadcrumbs, 2 tablespoons plain flour, 1 teaspoon garlic powder, 1 teaspoon smoked paprika, 2 eggs (beaten), salt, pepper

Instructions:

1. Preheat your air fryer to 190°C (375°F).
2. In one bowl, mix breadcrumbs, garlic powder, paprika, salt, and pepper. In another, add the flour.
3. Coat the mushroom strips in flour, dip them in beaten egg, then coat with the seasoned breadcrumb mixture.
4. Place the mushroom strips in the air fryer basket in a single layer.
5. Air fry for 810 minutes, shaking halfway through, until golden and crispy.
6. Serve with a lemon wedge and a side of garlic mayo for dipping.

Nutritional Info: Calories: 150 | Fat: 7g | Carbs: 16g | Protein: 4g

SWEET POTATO CRISPS

Prep: 5 mins | **Cook:** 12 mins | **Serves:** 4
Cooking Function: Air Fry

Ingredients:

UK: 2 medium sweet potatoes (thinly sliced), 1 tablespoon olive oil, salt, pepper

US: 2 medium sweet potatoes (thinly sliced), 1 tablespoon olive oil, salt, pepper

Instructions:

1. Preheat your air fryer to 180°C (350°F).
2. Toss the thinly sliced sweet potatoes in olive oil, salt, and pepper.
3. Spread the slices in a single layer in the air fryer basket.
4. Air fry for 1012 minutes, shaking halfway through, until crispy.
5. Let cool slightly before serving for extra crunch.

Nutritional Info: Calories: 110 | Fat: 3g | Carbs: 20g | Protein: 2g

ONION BHAJIS

Prep: 15 mins | **Cook:** 12 mins | **Serves:** 4

Cooking Function: Air Fry

Ingredients:

UK: 2 large onions (thinly sliced), 100g chickpea flour, 1 teaspoon cumin seeds, 1 teaspoon turmeric, 1 teaspoon ground coriander, 1 teaspoon chilli powder, 2 tablespoons water, salt

US: 2 large onions (thinly sliced), 1 cup chickpea flour, 1 teaspoon cumin seeds, 1 teaspoon turmeric, 1 teaspoon ground coriander, 1 teaspoon chilli powder, 2 tablespoons water, salt

Instructions:

1. Preheat your air fryer to 180°C (350°F).
2. In a bowl, mix the chickpea flour with the spices and water to form a thick batter.
3. Add the sliced onions and stir until well-coated.
4. Scoop spoonfuls of the mixture into the air fryer basket, flattening slightly.
5. Air fry for 10-12 minutes, turning halfway through, until golden and crispy.
6. Serve hot with chutney or yoghurt dip.

Nutritional Info: Calories: 140 | Fat: 4g | Carbs: 22g | Protein: 4g

ZUCCHINI CHIPS

Prep: 10 mins | **Cook:** 10 mins | **Serves:** 4

Cooking Function: Air Fry

Ingredients:

UK: 2 medium courgettes (thinly sliced), 50g breadcrumbs, 30g Parmesan cheese (grated), 1 teaspoon garlic powder, 1 egg (beaten), salt, pepper

US: 2 medium zucchinis (thinly sliced), ½ cup breadcrumbs, ¼ cup Parmesan cheese (grated), 1 teaspoon garlic powder, 1 egg (beaten), salt, pepper

Instructions:

1. Preheat your air fryer to 190°C (375°F).
2. In one bowl, mix breadcrumbs, Parmesan, garlic powder, salt, and pepper.
3. Dip each zucchini slice in beaten egg, then coat with the breadcrumb mixture.
4. Place the zucchini chips in the air fryer basket in a single layer.
5. Air fry for 8-10 minutes, turning halfway through, until crispy and golden.
6. Serve with a side of marinara sauce for dipping.

Nutritional Info: Calories: 120 | Fat: 6g | Carbs: 13g | Protein: 5g

SPINACH AND ARTICHOKE ROLLS

Prep: 15 mins | **Cook:** 10 mins | **Serves:** 4

Cooking Function: Air Fry

Ingredients:

UK: 1 sheet puff pastry, 100g spinach (chopped), 100g artichoke hearts (chopped), 50g cream cheese, 30g Parmesan cheese (grated), 1 egg (beaten), salt, pepper

US: 1 sheet puff pastry, 4 oz spinach (chopped), 4 oz artichoke hearts (chopped), 2 oz cream cheese, ¼ cup Parmesan cheese (grated), 1 egg (beaten), salt, pepper

Instructions:

1. Preheat your air fryer to 180°C (350°F).
2. In a bowl, mix the spinach, artichoke hearts, cream cheese, Parmesan, salt, and pepper.
3. Roll out the puff pastry and cut it into 4 squares.
4. Spoon the spinach artichoke mixture onto each square and roll them up.
5. Brush with beaten egg and place them in the air fryer basket.
6. Air fry for 8-10 minutes, until golden and puffed.
7. Serve warm with your favourite dip.

Nutritional Info: Calories: 200 | Fat: 12g | Carbs: 18g | Protein: 5g

CORN RIBLETS

Prep: 10 mins | **Cook:** 12 mins | **Serves:** 4

Cooking Function: Air Fry

Ingredients:

UK: 2 ears of corn (cut into quarters), 1 tablespoon olive oil, 1 teaspoon smoked paprika, salt, pepper

US: 2 ears of corn (cut into quarters), 1 tablespoon olive oil, 1 teaspoon smoked paprika, salt, pepper

Instructions:

1. Preheat your air fryer to 200°C (390°F).
2. Toss the corn riblets in olive oil, smoked paprika, salt, and pepper.
3. Place the riblets in the air fryer basket and air fry for 10-12 minutes, shaking halfway through, until golden and slightly charred.
4. Serve hot with a squeeze of lime for added flavour.

Nutritional Info: Calories: 90 | Fat: 4g | Carbs: 14g | Protein: 2g

BUFFALO CAULIFLOWER BITES

Prep: 15 mins | **Cook:** 20 mins | **Serves:** 4
Cooking Function: Air Fry

Ingredients:

UK: 1 medium cauliflower (cut into florets), 100g plain flour, 100ml water, 50ml hot sauce, 2 tablespoons butter (melted), salt, pepper

US: 1 medium cauliflower (cut into florets), ½ cup plain flour, ½ cup water, ¼ cup hot sauce, 2 tablespoons butter (melted), salt, pepper

Instructions:

1. Preheat your air fryer to 200°C (390°F).
2. In a bowl, whisk together flour, water, salt, and pepper to make a smooth batter.
3. Coat each cauliflower floret in the batter and place them in the air fryer.
4. Air fry for 15 minutes, shaking halfway through, until golden and crispy.
5. Toss the crispy cauliflower bites in a mixture of hot sauce and melted butter.
6. Return to the air fryer for an additional 5 minutes to set the sauce.
7. Serve with a side of blue cheese dressing or ranch.

Nutritional Info: Calories: 160 | Fat: 7g | Carbs: 20g | Protein: 4g

CRISPY OKRA FRIES

Prep: 10 mins | **Cook:** 10 mins | **Serves:** 4

Cooking Function: Air Fry

Ingredients:

UK: 200g okra (sliced), 50g cornmeal, 1 teaspoon paprika, salt, pepper, 1 tablespoon olive oil

US: 7 oz okra (sliced), ½ cup cornmeal, 1 teaspoon paprika, salt, pepper, 1 tablespoon olive oil

Instructions:

1. Preheat your air fryer to 190°C (375°F).
2. Toss the sliced okra in olive oil, cornmeal, paprika, salt, and pepper.
3. Spread the okra in a single layer in the air fryer basket.
4. Air fry for 810 minutes, shaking halfway through, until crispy and golden.
5. Serve immediately as a crunchy snack or side dish.

Nutritional Info: Calories: 100 | Fat: 4g | Carbs: 15g | Protein: 2g

CHAPTER 3: VEGETABLES MADE EASY

PERFECT ROASTED BROCCOLI

Prep: 5 mins | **Cook:** 10 mins | **Serves:** 4

Cooking Function: Air Fry

Ingredients:

UK: 400g broccoli florets, 15ml olive oil, 1 teaspoon garlic powder, salt, pepper

US: 14 oz broccoli florets, 1 tablespoon olive oil, 1 teaspoon garlic powder, salt, pepper

Instructions:

1. Preheat your air fryer to 200°C (390°F).
2. In a bowl, toss the broccoli florets with olive oil, garlic powder, salt, and pepper until evenly coated.
3. Place the florets in the air fryer basket in a single layer.
4. Air fry for 8-10 minutes, shaking the basket halfway through, until tender and slightly crispy.
5. Serve hot as a delicious side dish.

Nutritional Info: Calories: 110 | Fat: 5g | Carbs: 12g | Protein: 4g

CRISPY BRUSSELS SPROUTS

Prep: 10 mins | **Cook:** 15 mins | **Serves:** 4

Cooking Function: Air Fry

Ingredients:

UK: 500g Brussels sprouts (trimmed and halved), 30ml olive oil, 1 teaspoon balsamic vinegar, salt, pepper

US: 1 lb Brussels sprouts (trimmed and halved), 2 tablespoons olive oil, 1 teaspoon balsamic vinegar, salt, pepper

Instructions:

1. Preheat your air fryer to 200°C (390°F).
2. In a bowl, combine the halved Brussels sprouts with olive oil, balsamic vinegar, salt, and pepper, tossing until well coated.
3. Arrange the sprouts in the air fryer basket in a single layer.
4. Air fry for 12-15 minutes, shaking the basket halfway through, until crispy and browned.
5. Serve warm, drizzled with extra balsamic if desired.

Nutritional Info: Calories: 120 | Fat: 8g | Carbs: 12g | Protein: 4g

CAULIFLOWER STEAKS

Prep: 10 mins | **Cook:** 20 mins | **Serves:** 2
Cooking Function: Air Fry
Ingredients:

UK: 1 large cauliflower (cut into 2cm thick steaks), 30ml olive oil, 1 teaspoon smoked paprika, salt, pepper

US: 1 large cauliflower (cut into ¾ inch thick steaks), 2 tablespoons olive oil, 1 teaspoon smoked paprika, salt, pepper

Instructions:

1. Preheat your air fryer to 200°C (390°F).
2. Brush both sides of the cauliflower steaks with olive oil and season with smoked paprika, salt, and pepper.
3. Place the steaks in the air fryer basket.
4. Air fry for 15-20 minutes, flipping halfway through, until golden brown and tender.
5. Serve with your choice of sauce or relish.

Nutritional Info: Calories: 150 | Fat: 10g | Carbs: 10g | Protein: 5g

STUFFED PORTOBELLO MUSHROOMS

Prep: 15 mins | **Cook:** 12 mins | **Serves:** 4
Cooking Function: Air Fry
Ingredients:

UK: 4 large portobello mushrooms, 100g cream cheese, 50g grated cheese, 30g breadcrumbs, 2 cloves garlic (minced), salt, pepper, fresh herbs (for garnish)

US: 4 large portobello mushrooms, 3.5 oz cream cheese, ½ cup grated cheese, ¼ cup breadcrumbs, 2 cloves garlic (minced), salt, pepper, fresh herbs (for garnish)

Instructions:

1. Preheat your air fryer to 180°C (360°F).
2. mix the cream cheese, grated cheese, breadcrumbs, garlic, salt, and pepper until well combined.
3. Stuff each portobello mushroom cap with the cheese mixture.
4. Place the stuffed mushrooms in the air fryer basket.
5. Air fry for 10-12 minutes until the mushrooms are tender and the topping is golden.
6. Garnish with fresh herbs before serving.

Nutritional Info: Calories: 200 | Fat: 15g | Carbs: 10g | Protein: 6g

SESAME GREEN BEANS

Prep: 5 mins | **Cook:** 10 mins | **Serves:** 4
Cooking Function: Air Fry
Ingredients:
UK: 400g green beans (trimmed), 15ml sesame oil, 1 tablespoon sesame seeds, salt, pepper
US: 14 oz green beans (trimmed), 1 tablespoon sesame oil, 1 tablespoon sesame seeds, salt, pepper
Instructions:
1. Preheat your air fryer to 200°C (390°F).
2. Toss the green beans with sesame oil, sesame seeds, salt, and pepper until well coated.
3. Place the beans in the air fryer basket.
4. Air fry for 810 minutes, shaking the basket halfway through, until tender and slightly crispy.
5. Serve as a flavorful side dish.

Nutritional Info: Calories: 100 | Fat: 5g | Carbs: 8g | Protein: 3g

HONEYGLAZED CARROTS

Prep: 10 mins | **Cook:** 15 mins | **Serves:** 4
Cooking Function: Air Fry
Ingredients:
UK: 500g carrots (peeled and sliced), 30ml honey, 30ml olive oil, salt, pepper
US: 1 lb carrots (peeled and sliced), 2 tablespoons honey, 2 tablespoons olive oil, salt, pepper
Instructions:
1. Preheat your air fryer to 200°C (390°F).
2. In a bowl, mix the carrots with honey, olive oil, salt, and pepper until coated.
3. Place the carrots in the air fryer basket.
4. Air fry for 1215 minutes, shaking halfway through, until tender and caramelized.
5. Serve warm, perfect as a sweet side dish.

Nutritional Info: Calories: 140 | Fat: 6g | Carbs: 20g | Protein: 2g

CRISPY KALE CHIPS

Prep: 5 mins | **Cook:** 8 mins | **Serves:** 4
Cooking Function: Air Fry
Ingredients:
UK: 200g kale (stems removed, torn into pieces), 15ml olive oil, salt, pepper
US: 7 oz kale (stems removed, torn into pieces), 1 tablespoon olive oil, salt, pepper
Instructions:
1. Preheat your air fryer to 180°C (360°F).
2. Toss the kale pieces with olive oil, salt, and pepper until evenly coated.
3. Place the kale in the air fryer basket in a single layer.
4. Air fry for 68 minutes, shaking halfway through, until crispy.
5. Enjoy them as a healthy snack!

Nutritional Info: Calories: 50 | Fat: 4g | Carbs: 6g | Protein: 2g

CORN ON THE COB

Prep: 5 mins | **Cook:** 12 mins | **Serves:** 4
Cooking Function: Air Fry
Ingredients:
UK: 4 corn cobs, 30ml butter (melted), salt, pepper
US: 4 corn cobs, 2 tablespoons butter (melted), salt, pepper
Instructions:
1. Preheat your air fryer to 200°C (390°F).
2. Brush the corn cobs with melted butter and sprinkle with salt and pepper.
3. Place the cobs in the air fryer basket.
4. Air fry for 1012 minutes, turning halfway through, until tender.
5. Serve hot, perfect for a summer BBQ.

Nutritional Info: Calories: 120 | Fat: 5g | Carbs: 18g | Protein: 4g

GARLIC PARMESAN ASPARAGUS

Prep: 5 mins | **Cook:** 10 mins | **Serves:** 4
Cooking Function: Air Fry
Ingredients:
UK: 400g asparagus spears, 30ml olive oil, 2 tablespoons grated Parmesan cheese, 2 cloves garlic (minced), salt, pepper
US: 14 oz asparagus spears, 2 tablespoons olive oil, 2 tablespoons grated Parmesan cheese, 2 cloves garlic (minced), salt, pepper
Instructions:
1. Preheat your air fryer to 200°C (390°F).
2. In a bowl, toss the asparagus with olive oil, Parmesan cheese, garlic, salt, and pepper until evenly coated.
3. Place the asparagus in the air fryer basket.
4. Air fry for 810 minutes, until tender and cheese is melted.
5. Serve warm, great as a side dish.
Nutritional Info: Calories: 130 | Fat: 10g | Carbs: 5g | Protein: 6g

MEDITERRANEAN AUBERGINE ROUNDS

Prep: 10 mins | **Cook:** 15 mins | **Serves:** 4
Cooking Function: Air Fry
Ingredients:
UK: 2 medium aubergines (sliced into 1cm rounds), 30ml olive oil, 1 teaspoon dried oregano, salt, pepper
US: 2 medium eggplants (sliced into ½ inch rounds), 2 tablespoons olive oil, 1 teaspoon dried oregano, salt, pepper
Instructions:
1. Preheat your air fryer to 200°C (390°F).
2. Brush both sides of the aubergine rounds with olive oil and season with oregano, salt, and pepper.
3. Place the rounds in the air fryer basket in a single layer.
4. Air fry for 1215 minutes, flipping halfway through, until golden brown.
5. Serve warm, ideal as an appetizer or side dish.
Nutritional Info: Calories: 100 | Fat: 7g | Carbs: 10g | Protein: 2g

CRISPY COURGETTE FRIES

Prep: 10 mins | **Cook:** 12 mins | **Serves:** 4

Cooking Function: Air Fry

Ingredients:

UK: 2 large courgettes (cut into fries), 30g breadcrumbs, 30g grated Parmesan cheese, 1 egg (beaten), salt, pepper

US: 2 large zucchini (cut into fries), 1 cup breadcrumbs, 1 cup grated Parmesan cheese, 1 egg (beaten), salt, pepper

Instructions:

1. Preheat your air fryer to 200°C (390°F).
2. Dip the courgette fries into the beaten egg, then coat in a mixture of breadcrumbs, Parmesan cheese, salt, and pepper.
3. Place the fries in the air fryer basket in a single layer.
4. Air fry for 10-12 minutes, shaking the basket halfway through, until golden and crispy.
5. Serve with your favourite dip for a tasty snack.

Nutritional Info: Calories: 170 | Fat: 9g | Carbs: 17g | Protein: 7g

SWEET AND SPICY BUTTERNUT SQUASH

Prep: 10 mins | **Cook:** 20 mins | **Serves:** 4

Cooking Function: Air Fry

Ingredients:

UK: 500g butternut squash (peeled and cubed), 30ml olive oil, 2 tablespoons maple syrup, 1 teaspoon cayenne pepper, salt

US: 1 lb butternut squash (peeled and cubed), 2 tablespoons olive oil, 2 tablespoons maple syrup, 1 teaspoon cayenne pepper, salt

Instructions:

1. Preheat your air fryer to 200°C (390°F).
2. In a bowl, toss the butternut squash with olive oil, maple syrup, cayenne pepper, and salt until well coated.
3. Place the squash in the air fryer basket.
4. Air fry for 15-20 minutes, shaking halfway through, until tender and caramelized.
5. Serve warm, perfect as a side dish.

Nutritional Info: Calories: 140 | Fat: 7g | Carbs: 19g | Protein: 2g

HERB ROASTED ROOT VEGETABLES

Prep: 10 mins | **Cook:** 25 mins | **Serves:** 4
Cooking Function: Air Fry

Ingredients:

UK: 400g mixed root vegetables (carrots, parsnips, potatoes), 30ml olive oil, 1 tablespoon mixed dried herbs, salt, pepper

US: 14 oz mixed root vegetables (carrots, parsnips, potatoes), 2 tablespoons olive oil, 1 tablespoon mixed dried herbs, salt, pepper

Instructions:

1. Preheat your air fryer to 200°C (390°F).
2. In a bowl, toss the root vegetables with olive oil, dried herbs, salt, and pepper until well coated.
3. Place the vegetables in the air fryer basket.
4. Air fry for 20-25 minutes, shaking the basket halfway through, until tender and golden.
5. Serve hot as a comforting side dish.

Nutritional Info: Calories: 150 | Fat: 8g | Carbs: 18g | Protein: 3g

CHAPTER 4: MAIN DISHES

CRISPY TOFU KATSU CURRY

Prep: 15 mins | **Cook:** 25 mins | **Serves:** 4
Cooking Function: Air Fry

Ingredients:

UK: 400g firm tofu (pressed and sliced), 100g panko breadcrumbs, 50g plain flour, 1 egg (or flax egg for vegan), 50ml soy sauce, 1 tablespoon curry powder, 100ml vegetable oil, salt to taste

US: 14oz firm tofu (pressed and sliced), 1 cup panko breadcrumbs, ⅓ cup all-purpose flour, 1 egg (or flax egg for vegan), 3 tablespoons soy sauce, 1 tablespoon curry powder, ⅓ cup vegetable oil, salt to taste

Instructions:

1. Start by preheating your air fryer to 200°C (400°F).
2. Prepare your tofu by slicing it into thick pieces. Pat them dry with kitchen paper to remove excess moisture.
3. Set up your breading station: one plate with flour mixed with salt, one with beaten egg (or flax egg), and one with panko breadcrumbs mixed with curry powder.
4. Dip each tofu slice first in the flour, then in the egg, and finally coat it in the panko mixture, pressing gently to ensure it's well covered.
5. Lightly spray the air fryer basket with oil, then arrange the breaded tofu slices in a single layer. Spray the tops with a bit more oil.
6. Air fry for about 1520 minutes until golden brown and crispy, flipping halfway through for even cooking.
7. While the tofu is cooking, prepare your curry sauce by heating a saucepan over medium heat and adding curry powder to taste, followed by your preferred curry sauce ingredients (like coconut milk or storebought sauce).
8. Serve the crispy tofu katsu drizzled with curry sauce, and enjoy this delicious dish from the Complete Vegetarian Air Fryer Cookbook New Edition!

Nutritional Info: Calories: 320 | Fat: 15g | Carbs: 30g | Protein: 20g

STUFFED BELL PEPPERS

Prep: 10 mins | **Cook:** 30 mins | **Serves:** 4
Cooking Function: Air Fry

Ingredients:

UK: 4 large bell peppers (halved and deseeded), 200g cooked quinoa, 150g black beans (drained), 100g corn, 1 teaspoon cumin, 50g grated cheese (optional), salt and pepper to taste

US: 4 large bell peppers (halved and deseeded), 1 cup cooked quinoa, 1 cup black beans (drained), ⅔ cup corn, 1 teaspoon cumin, ½ cup grated cheese (optional), salt and pepper to taste

Instructions:

1. Preheat your air fryer to 180°C (356°F).
2. In a large bowl, combine the cooked quinoa, black beans, corn, cumin, salt, and pepper. Mix well.
3. Fill each bell pepper half generously with the quinoa mixture, packing it down lightly. If using cheese, sprinkle it on top.
4. Arrange the stuffed peppers in the air fryer basket.
5. Air fry for 25-30 minutes until the peppers are tender and the filling is heated through.
6. Serve the stuffed bell peppers hot, and enjoy a tasty, filling dish from the Complete Vegetarian Air Fryer Cookbook New Edition!

Nutritional Info: Calories: 260 | Fat: 8g | Carbs: 43g | Protein: 12g

EGGPLANT PARMESAN

Prep: 20 mins | **Cook:** 20 mins | **Serves:** 4

Cooking Function: Air Fry

Ingredients:

UK: 2 medium eggplants (sliced), 200g marinara sauce, 100g mozzarella cheese (grated), 50g Parmesan cheese (grated), 100g breadcrumbs, 1 egg (or flax egg for vegan), 50ml olive oil, salt, and pepper to taste

US: 2 medium eggplants (sliced), 1 cup marinara sauce, 1 cup mozzarella cheese (grated), ½ cup Parmesan cheese (grated), 1 cup breadcrumbs, 1 egg (or flax egg for vegan), ⅓ cup olive oil, salt, and pepper to taste

Instructions:

1. Preheat your air fryer to 200°C (400°F).
2. Sprinkle the eggplant slices with salt and let them sit for about 10 minutes to draw out moisture. Rinse and pat dry.
3. Set up a breading station: one bowl with breadcrumbs, and one with beaten egg (or flax egg).
4. Dip each eggplant slice in the egg, then coat it in breadcrumbs.
5. Lightly spray the air fryer basket with olive oil and arrange the breaded eggplant slices in a single layer.
6. Air fry for 10 minutes, then flip and air fry for an additional 510 minutes until golden.
7. In a baking dish, layer the marinara sauce, eggplant slices, mozzarella, and Parmesan. Repeat until all ingredients are used.
8. Air fry for another 510 minutes until the cheese is melted and bubbly. Serve hot from the Complete Vegetarian Air Fryer Cookbook New Edition!

Nutritional Info: Calories: 330 | Fat: 22g | Carbs: 30g | Protein: 12g

CAULIFLOWER STEAK BURGER

Prep: 15 mins | **Cook:** 20 mins | **Serves:** 2
Cooking Function: Air Fry
Ingredients:
UK: 1 large cauliflower (cut into 2 thick steaks), 30ml olive oil, 1 teaspoon garlic powder, 1 teaspoon smoked paprika, salt and pepper to taste, 2 burger buns, lettuce, tomato, and your choice of condiments
US: 1 large cauliflower (cut into 2 thick steaks), 2 tablespoons olive oil, 1 teaspoon garlic powder, 1 teaspoon smoked paprika, salt and pepper to taste, 2 burger buns, lettuce, tomato, and your choice of condiments
Instructions:
1. Preheat your air fryer to 200°C (400°F).
2. Brush both sides of the cauliflower steaks with olive oil and season with garlic powder, smoked paprika, salt, and pepper.
3. Place the cauliflower steaks in the air fryer basket and air fry for 10 minutes.
4. Carefully flip the steaks and air fry for an additional 510 minutes until golden and tender.
5. Serve the cauliflower steaks in burger buns with lettuce, tomato, and your favourite condiments from the Complete Vegetarian Air Fryer Cookbook New Edition!

Nutritional Info: Calories: 220 | Fat: 14g | Carbs: 24g | Protein: 5g

QUINOA AND BLACK BEAN PATTIES

Prep: 10 mins | **Cook:** 15 mins | **Serves:** 4
Cooking Function: Air Fry
Ingredients:
UK: 200g cooked quinoa, 150g black beans (drained), 50g breadcrumbs, 1 egg (or flax egg for vegan), 1 teaspoon cumin, 1 teaspoon garlic powder, salt and pepper to taste
US: 1 cup cooked quinoa, 1 cup black beans (drained), ½ cup breadcrumbs, 1 egg (or flax egg for vegan), 1 teaspoon cumin, 1 teaspoon garlic powder, salt and pepper to taste

Instructions:

1. Preheat your air fryer to 200°C (400°F).
2. In a bowl, combine cooked quinoa, black beans, breadcrumbs, egg (or flax egg), cumin, garlic powder, salt, and pepper. Mix until well combined.
3. Form the mixture into patties of your desired size.
4. Lightly spray the air fryer basket with oil and place the patties in a single layer.
5. Air fry for 10-15 minutes until golden and crispy, flipping halfway through.
6. Serve the patties hot, and enjoy this protein-packed recipe from the Complete Vegetarian Air Fryer Cookbook New Edition!

Nutritional Info: Calories: 210 | Fat: 4g | Carbs: 35g | Protein: 10g

MEDITERRANEAN STUFFED COURGETTES

Prep: 15 mins | **Cook:** 20 mins | **Serves:** 4

Cooking Function: Air Fry

Ingredients:

UK: 4 courgettes (halved and hollowed), 200g cherry tomatoes (halved), 100g feta cheese (crumbled), 50g olives (chopped), 1 tablespoon olive oil, salt and pepper to taste

US: 4 zucchinis (halved and hollowed), 1 cup cherry tomatoes (halved), ⅓ cup feta cheese (crumbled), ⅓ cup olives (chopped), 2 tablespoons olive oil, salt and pepper to taste

Instructions:

1. Preheat your air fryer to 180°C (356°F).
2. In a bowl, mix the cherry tomatoes, feta cheese, olives, olive oil, salt, and pepper.
3. Fill each courgette half with the mixture, packing it in gently.
4. Arrange the stuffed courgettes in the air fryer basket.
5. Air fry for about 15-20 minutes until the courgettes are tender and the filling is warmed through.
6. Serve the Mediterranean stuffed courgettes as a fresh, vibrant dish from the Complete Vegetarian Air Fryer Cookbook New Edition!

Nutritional Info: Calories: 180 | Fat: 11g | Carbs: 14g | Protein: 6g

CRISPY TEMPEH BUDDHA BOWL

Prep: 15 mins | **Cook:** 20 mins | **Serves:** 4

Cooking Function: Air Fry

Ingredients:

UK: 200g tempeh (sliced), 30ml soy sauce, 20ml maple syrup, 1 teaspoon garlic powder, 100g cooked brown rice, 100g mixed greens, 50g avocado (sliced), sesame seeds for garnish

US: 7oz tempeh (sliced), 2 tablespoons soy sauce, 1 tablespoon maple syrup, 1 teaspoon garlic powder, 1 cup cooked brown rice, 1 cup mixed greens, ½ avocado (sliced), sesame seeds for garnish

Instructions:

1. Preheat your air fryer to 200°C (400°F).
2. In a bowl, marinate the tempeh slices with soy sauce, maple syrup, and garlic powder for about 10 minutes.
3. Place the marinated tempeh in the air fryer basket and air fry for 1015 minutes until crispy and golden.
4. To assemble, serve the crispy tempeh over cooked brown rice, topped with mixed greens, sliced avocado, and a sprinkle of sesame seeds.
5. Enjoy this nourishing bowl from the Complete Vegetarian Air Fryer Cookbook New Edition!

Nutritional Info: Calories: 350 | Fat: 20g | Carbs: 32g | Protein: 12g

VEGETABLE LASAGNA ROLLUPS

Prep: 20 mins | **Cook:** 25 mins | **Serves:** 4

Cooking Function: Air Fry

Ingredients:

UK: 8 lasagna noodles (cooked), 200g ricotta cheese, 100g spinach (wilted), 150g marinara sauce, 50g mozzarella cheese (grated), salt and pepper to taste

US: 8 lasagna noodles (cooked), 7oz ricotta cheese, 3.5oz spinach (wilted), 1 cup marinara sauce, ½ cup mozzarella cheese (grated), salt and pepper to taste

Instructions:
1. Preheat your air fryer to 180°C (356°F).
2. In a bowl, mix ricotta cheese, wilted spinach, salt, and pepper.
3. Spread some marinara sauce on the bottom of a baking dish.
4. Take a lasagna noodle, fill it with the ricotta mixture, and roll it up tightly.
5. Place the rollups seam side down in the baking dish, and top with remaining marinara sauce and mozzarella cheese.
6. Air fry for 20-25 minutes until heated through and the cheese is bubbly.
7. Serve warm, enjoying the layers of flavour from the Complete Vegetarian Air Fryer Cookbook New Edition!

Nutritional Info: Calories: 320 | Fat: 14g | Carbs: 36g | Protein: 18g

TOFU FISH AND CHIPS

Prep: 15 mins | **Cook:** 25 mins | **Serves:** 4
Cooking Function: Air Fry

Ingredients:
UK: 400g firm tofu (pressed and sliced into fishlike pieces), 100g flour, 100ml beer (or sparkling water), 100g breadcrumbs, 30ml tartar sauce (for serving), salt and pepper to taste

US: 14oz firm tofu (pressed and sliced into fishlike pieces), ⅔ cup flour, ⅓ cup beer (or sparkling water), 1 cup breadcrumbs, 2 tablespoons tartar sauce (for serving), salt and pepper to taste

Instructions:
1. Preheat your air fryer to 200°C (400°F).
2. Pat the tofu slices dry and season with salt and pepper.
3. In a bowl, mix flour with a bit of salt, then gradually whisk in beer (or sparkling water) until smooth.
4. Dip each tofu slice into the batter, then coat with breadcrumbs.
5. Lightly spray the air fryer basket with oil and arrange the battered tofu slices in a single layer.
6. Air fry for about 15-20 minutes until golden and crispy, flipping halfway through.
7. Serve with tartar sauce for dipping, enjoying this plant-based twist on a classic dish from the Complete Vegetarian Air Fryer Cookbook New Edition!

Nutritional Info: Calories: 290 | Fat: 8g | Carbs: 38g | Protein: 15g

STUFFED POTATO SKINS

Prep: 15 mins | **Cook:** 20 mins | **Serves:** 4
Cooking Function: Air Fry

Ingredients:

UK: 4 medium potatoes (baked and halved), 100g cheddar cheese (grated), 50g sour cream, 100g cooked bacon bits (or plant-based alternative), spring onions for garnish

US: 4 medium potatoes (baked and halved), 1 cup cheddar cheese (grated), ¼ cup sour cream, ⅔ cup cooked bacon bits (or plant-based alternative), green onions for garnish

Instructions:

1. Preheat your air fryer to 200°C (400°F).
2. Carefully scoop out the flesh from each potato half, leaving a thin layer for structure.
3. In a bowl, mix the scooped potato, cheddar cheese, sour cream, and bacon bits (or alternative). Season with salt and pepper.
4. Fill each potato skin with the mixture and place them in the air fryer basket.
5. Air fry for 15-20 minutes until the cheese is melted and the skins are crispy.
6. Garnish with chopped spring onions and serve as a delightful appetizer from the Complete Vegetarian Air Fryer Cookbook New Edition!

Nutritional Info: Calories: 340 | Fat: 20g | Carbs: 30g | Protein: 10g

CHICKPEA AND SPINACH PATTIES

Prep: 10 mins | **Cook:** 15 mins | **Serves:** 4

Cooking Function: Air Fry

Ingredients:

UK: 200g canned chickpeas (drained), 100g fresh spinach (chopped), 50g breadcrumbs, 1 egg (or flax egg for vegan), 1 teaspoon cumin, salt and pepper to taste

US: 1 cup canned chickpeas (drained), 3.5oz fresh spinach (chopped), ½ cup breadcrumbs, 1 egg (or flax egg for vegan), 1 teaspoon cumin, salt and pepper to taste

Instructions:

1. Preheat your air fryer to 200°C (400°F).
2. In a bowl, mash the chickpeas with a fork until slightly chunky.
3. Add chopped spinach, breadcrumbs, egg (or flax egg), cumin, salt, and pepper. Mix until combined.
4. Form the mixture into small patties.
5. Lightly spray the air fryer basket with oil and place the patties in a single layer.
6. Air fry for about 1015 minutes until crispy and golden, flipping halfway through.
7. Serve the chickpea and spinach patties warm, enjoying their flavour-packed goodness from the Complete Vegetarian Air Fryer Cookbook New Edition!

Nutritional Info: Calories: 210 | Fat: 5g | Carbs: 30g | Protein: 10g

MUSHROOM WELLINGTON

Prep: 30 mins | **Cook:** 25 mins | **Serves:** 4

Cooking Function: Air Fry

Ingredients:

UK: 400g mushrooms (finely chopped), 1 onion (finely chopped), 2 garlic cloves (minced), 200g puff pastry, 1 egg (for egg wash), salt and pepper to taste

US: 14oz mushrooms (finely chopped), 1 onion (finely chopped), 2 garlic cloves (minced), 7oz puff pastry, 1 egg (for egg wash), salt and pepper to taste

Instructions:
1. Preheat your air fryer to 200°C (400°F).
2. In a pan, sauté the onions and garlic until translucent, then add the mushrooms and cook until moisture has evaporated. Season with salt and pepper.
3. Roll out the puff pastry and place the mushroom mixture in the centre. Fold the pastry over to enclose the filling and seal the edges.
4. Brush the top with the beaten egg for a golden finish.
5. Place the Wellington in the air fryer basket.
6. Air fry for 20-25 minutes until golden brown and flaky. Serve warm, enjoying this elegant dish from the Complete Vegetarian Air Fryer Cookbook New Edition!

Nutritional Info: Calories: 320 | Fat: 20g | Carbs: 30g | Protein: 6g

LENTIL AND VEGETABLE LOAF

Prep: 20 mins | Cook: 45 mins | Serves: 6

Cooking Function: Bake

Ingredients:

UK: 200g lentils (cooked), 1 onion (finely chopped), 1 carrot (grated), 50g breadcrumbs, 1 teaspoon thyme, salt and pepper to taste

US: 1 cup lentils (cooked), 1 onion (finely chopped), 1 carrot (grated), ½ cup breadcrumbs, 1 teaspoon thyme, salt and pepper to taste

Instructions:
1. Preheat your air fryer to 180°C (356°F).
2. In a bowl, combine cooked lentils, chopped onion, grated carrots, breadcrumbs, thyme, salt, and pepper.
3. Shape the mixture into a loaf and place it in a baking dish that fits your air fryer.
4. Bake for about 40-45 minutes until firm and heated through.
5. Serve slices of the lentil and vegetable loaf warm, enjoying its hearty goodness from the Complete Vegetarian Air Fryer Cookbook New Edition!

Nutritional Info: Calories: 240 | Fat: 4g | Carbs: 45g | Protein: 14g

CHAPTER 5: GLOBAL FLAVOURS

INDIAN SAMOSAS

Prep: 20 mins | **Cook:** 15 mins | **Serves:** 4
Cooking Function: Air Fry
Ingredients:

UK: 250g potatoes (peeled and cubed), 100g frozen peas, 1 teaspoon cumin seeds, 1 teaspoon garam masala, 30g fresh coriander (chopped), 4 sheets of readymade pastry, 1 tablespoon oil, salt to taste

US: 1 medium potato (peeled and cubed), ⅔ cup frozen peas, 1 teaspoon cumin seeds, 1 teaspoon garam masala, ¼ cup fresh coriander (chopped), 4 sheets of readymade pastry, 1 tablespoon oil, salt to taste

Instructions:
1. Preheat your air fryer to 200°C (400°F).
2. Boil the cubed potatoes in salted water until tender, then drain and mash.
3. In a pan, heat a bit of oil and toast cumin seeds until fragrant. Add peas, garam masala, and chopped coriander; mix in the mashed potatoes. Season to taste.
4. Cut the pastry sheets in half. Place a spoonful of filling in each half and fold into triangles. Seal the edges with a little water.
5. Brush the samosas lightly with oil and place them in the air fryer basket.
6. Air fry for 1215 minutes until golden and crispy. Serve with chutney!

Nutritional Info: Calories: 220 | Fat: 6g | Carbs: 34g | Protein: 5g

MEXICAN BEAN AND CHEESE TAQUITOS

Prep: 10 mins | **Cook:** 10 mins | **Serves:** 4
Cooking Function: Air Fry
Ingredients:

UK: 8 small corn tortillas, 200g black beans (cooked and mashed), 100g grated cheese, 1 teaspoon cumin, 1 tablespoon fresh cilantro (chopped), 30ml oil, salt to taste

US: 8 small corn tortillas, 1 cup black beans (cooked and mashed), 1 cup grated cheese, 1 teaspoon cumin, 1 tablespoon fresh cilantro (chopped), 2 tablespoons oil, salt to taste

Instructions:

1. Preheat your air fryer to 200°C (400°F).
2. In a bowl, mix the mashed beans, cheese, cumin, cilantro, and salt until well combined.
3. Lightly warm the tortillas to make them pliable.
4. Spoon the filling onto one end of each tortilla, roll tightly, and secure with a toothpick if needed.
5. Brush with oil and place in the air fryer basket.
6. Air fry for 8-10 minutes until crispy and golden. Serve with salsa!

Nutritional Info: Calories: 180 | Fat: 8g | Carbs: 24g | Protein: 7g

ITALIAN ARANCINI BALLS

Prep: 15 mins | **Cook:** 20 mins | **Serves:** 4

Cooking Function: Air Fry

Ingredients:

UK: 300g cooked risotto rice, 50g mozzarella (cubed), 30g grated Parmesan cheese, 100g breadcrumbs, 1 egg, 1 teaspoon dried oregano, oil spray

US: 1.5 cups cooked risotto rice, 2oz mozzarella (cubed), ¼ cup grated Parmesan cheese, ½ cup breadcrumbs, 1 egg, 1 teaspoon dried oregano, oil spray

Instructions:

1. Preheat your air fryer to 200°C (400°F).
2. In a bowl, combine the risotto rice, mozzarella, Parmesan, egg, and oregano.
3. Shape the mixture into small balls and roll them in breadcrumbs to coat.
4. Spray the arancini with oil and place it in the air fryer basket.
5. Air fry for 15-20 minutes until golden and crispy. Serve with marinara sauce!

Nutritional Info: Calories: 300 | Fat: 10g | Carbs: 38g | Protein: 10g

GREEK SPANAKOPITA

Prep: 15 mins | **Cook:** 15 mins | **Serves:** 4
Cooking Function: Bake
Ingredients:
UK: 200g spinach (fresh or frozen), 100g feta cheese (crumbled), 1 onion (finely chopped), 1 clove garlic (minced), 4 sheets of filo pastry, 30g melted butter, salt and pepper to taste
US: 7oz spinach (fresh or frozen), 3.5oz feta cheese (crumbled), 1 onion (finely chopped), 1 clove garlic (minced), 4 sheets of phyllo pastry, 2 tablespoons melted butter, salt and pepper to taste
Instructions:
1. Preheat your air fryer to 180°C (356°F).
2. In a pan, sauté onion and garlic until soft, then add spinach until wilted.
3. Mix in the feta, and season with salt and pepper.
4. Lay a sheet of filo pastry, brush with melted butter, and layer another sheet on top.
5. Spoon the spinach mixture at one end and roll tightly to form a log.
6. Brush with butter and place in the air fryer. Air fry for 12-15 minutes until golden and crisp.

Nutritional Info: Calories: 250 | Fat: 16g | Carbs: 20g | Protein: 7g

JAPANESE TEMPURA VEGETABLES

Prep: 15 mins | **Cook:** 10 mins | **Serves:** 4
Cooking Function: Air Fry
Ingredients:
UK: 150g mixed vegetables (e.g., broccoli, sweet potato, bell peppers), 75g plain flour, 1 egg, 150ml cold water, 1 teaspoon baking powder, salt to taste
US: 5oz mixed vegetables (e.g., broccoli, sweet potato, bell peppers), ½ cup all-purpose flour, 1 egg, ½ cup cold water, 1 teaspoon baking powder, salt to taste
Instructions:
1. Preheat your air fryer to 200°C (400°F).
2. In a bowl, mix the flour, egg, water, baking powder, and salt until a batter forms.
3. Dip the vegetable pieces into the batter, coating them well.
4. Arrange the coated vegetables in the air fryer basket in a single layer.
5. Air fry for 8-10 minutes until crispy and golden. Serve with dipping sauce!

Nutritional Info: Calories: 180 | Fat: 5g | Carbs: 30g | Protein: 5g

THAI SPRING ROLLS

Prep: 20 mins | **Cook:** 10 mins | **Serves:** 4

Cooking Function: Air Fry

Ingredients:

UK: 100g rice noodles, 1 carrot (julienned), 100g cabbage (shredded), 1 bell pepper (sliced), 8 rice paper wrappers, 1 tablespoon soy sauce, oil spray

US: 3.5oz rice noodles, 1 carrot (julienned), 3.5oz cabbage (shredded), 1 bell pepper (sliced), 8 rice paper wrappers, 1 tablespoon soy sauce, oil spray

Instructions:

1. Preheat your air fryer to 200°C (400°F).
2. Soak the rice noodles in hot water until soft, then drain and mix with vegetables and soy sauce.
3. Soak each rice paper wrapper in warm water until pliable.
4. Place a spoonful of filling in the centre, fold the sides, and roll tightly.
5. Spray the spring rolls with oil and arrange them in the air fryer basket.
6. Air fry for 8-10 minutes until golden and crispy. Serve with sweet chilli sauce!

Nutritional Info: Calories: 150 | Fat: 4g | Carbs: 25g | Protein: 5g

MIDDLE EASTERN FALAFEL

Prep: 15 mins | **Cook:** 15 mins | **Serves:** 4

Cooking Function: Air Fry

Ingredients:

UK: 200g chickpeas (soaked overnight), 1 onion (chopped), 2 cloves garlic (minced), 1 teaspoon cumin, 1 teaspoon coriander, 30g parsley (chopped), 1 tablespoon flour, oil spray

US: 1 cup chickpeas (soaked overnight), 1 onion (chopped), 2 cloves garlic (minced), 1 teaspoon cumin, 1 teaspoon coriander, ¼ cup parsley (chopped), 1 tablespoon flour, oil spray

Instructions:

1. Preheat your air fryer to 200°C (400°F).
2. In a food processor, blend chickpeas, onion, garlic, spices, and parsley until coarse.
3. Add flour and mix well. Shape into small balls or patties.
4. Spray the falafel with oil and arrange in the air fryer basket.
5. Air fry for 12-15 minutes until golden and crispy. Serve with tahini sauce!

Nutritional Info: Calories: 250 | Fat: 8g | Carbs: 35g | Protein: 10g

CHINESE SALT AND PEPPER TOFU

Prep: 15 mins | **Cook:** 15 mins | **Serves:** 4
Cooking Function: Air Fry
Ingredients:

UK: 400g firm tofu (pressed and cubed), 30g cornstarch, 1 teaspoon salt, 1 teaspoon black pepper, 1 tablespoon soy sauce, 1 spring onion (sliced)

US: 14oz firm tofu (pressed and cubed), ¼ cup cornstarch, 1 teaspoon salt, 1 teaspoon black pepper, 1 tablespoon soy sauce, 1 green onion (sliced)

Instructions:
1. Preheat your air fryer to 200°C (400°F).
2. In a bowl, toss the tofu cubes with cornstarch, salt, and pepper until evenly coated.
3. Drizzle with soy sauce and toss again.
4. Place the tofu in a single layer in the air fryer basket.
5. Air fry for 12-15 minutes until golden and crispy, shaking halfway through. Garnish with spring onion and serve!

Nutritional Info: Calories: 200 | Fat: 10g | Carbs: 12g | Protein: 18g

VIETNAMESE BANH MI ROLLS

Prep: 20 mins | **Cook:** 10 mins | **Serves:** 4
Cooking Function: Bake
Ingredients:

UK: 4 baguette rolls, 200g marinated tofu, 100g pickled carrots and daikon, 1 cucumber (sliced), fresh coriander, 30ml soy sauce

US: 4 baguette rolls, 7oz marinated tofu, 1 cup pickled carrots and daikon, 1 cucumber (sliced), fresh cilantro, 2 tablespoons soy sauce

Instructions:
1. Preheat your air fryer to 180°C (356°F).
2. Slice the baguette rolls open but not all the way through.
3. Fill each roll with marinated tofu, pickled vegetables, cucumber slices, and fresh coriander.
4. Brush the outside of the rolls with soy sauce.
5. Place in the air fryer basket and bake for 8-10 minutes until crispy. Enjoy!

Nutritional Info: Calories: 320 | Fat: 9g | Carbs: 50g | Protein: 14g

KOREAN KIMCHI PANCAKES

Prep: 15 mins | **Cook:** 10 mins | **Serves:** 4

Cooking Function: Air Fry

Ingredients:

UK: 200g kimchi (chopped), 150g plain flour, 1 egg, 100ml water, 1 spring onion (sliced), oil spray

US: 7oz kimchi (chopped), 1 cup all-purpose flour, 1 egg, ⅓ cup water, 1 green onion (sliced), oil spray

Instructions:

1. Preheat your air fryer to 200°C (400°F).
2. In a bowl, mix the kimchi, flour, egg, and water until combined.
3. Stir in the sliced spring onion.
4. Spray the air fryer basket with oil, then pour in the batter to form pancakes.
5. Air fry for 8-10 minutes until golden and crispy. Cut into wedges and serve with soy sauce!

Nutritional Info: Calories: 220 | Fat: 8g | Carbs: 32g | Protein: 6g

ETHIOPIAN LENTIL SAMBUSAS

Prep: 20 mins | **Cook:** 15 mins | **Serves:** 4

Cooking Function: Air Fry

Ingredients:

UK: 150g lentils (cooked), 1 onion (finely chopped), 1 teaspoon cumin, 1 teaspoon turmeric, 1 tablespoon oil, 4 sheets of pastry, salt to taste

US: 1 cup lentils (cooked), 1 onion (finely chopped), 1 teaspoon cumin, 1 teaspoon turmeric, 1 tablespoon oil, 4 sheets of pastry, salt to taste

Instructions:

1. Preheat your air fryer to 200°C (400°F).
2. In a pan, heat oil and sauté the onion until translucent. Add lentils, cumin, turmeric, and salt; cook for a few minutes.
3. Cut the pastry sheets in half, place a spoonful of filling in each half, and fold to seal.
4. Brush the sambusas with oil and arrange in the air fryer basket.
5. Air fry for 12-15 minutes until golden. Serve hot!

Nutritional Info: Calories: 250 | Fat: 9g | Carbs: 35g | Protein: 12g

RUSSIAN POTATO VARENIKI

Prep: 30 mins | **Cook:** 15 mins | **Serves:** 4

Cooking Function: Bake

Ingredients:

UK: 300g potatoes (boiled and mashed), 200g flour, 1 egg, 30ml water, salt to taste

US: 2 cups potatoes (boiled and mashed), 1½ cups flour, 1 egg, 2 tablespoons water, salt to taste

Instructions:

1. Preheat your air fryer to 180°C (356°F).
2. In a bowl, mix the flour, egg, water, and salt to form a dough.
3. Roll out the dough and cut into circles. Fill each with mashed potatoes, fold, and seal the edges.
4. Place the vareniki in the air fryer basket.
5. Air fry for 1215 minutes until golden and cooked through. Serve with sour cream!

Nutritional Info: Calories: 290 | Fat: 6g | Carbs: 52g | Protein: 9g

LEBANESE SPINACH FATAYER

Prep: 15 mins | **Cook:** 15 mins | **Serves:** 4

Cooking Function: Bake

Ingredients:

UK: 250g spinach (fresh), 100g feta cheese (crumbled), 1 onion (chopped), 4 sheets of pastry, 30ml olive oil, salt and pepper to taste

US: 9oz spinach (fresh), 3.5oz feta cheese (crumbled), 1 onion (chopped), 4 sheets of pastry, 2 tablespoons olive oil, salt and pepper to taste

Instructions:

1. Preheat your air fryer to 200°C (400°F).
2. Sauté the onion until soft, then add the spinach until wilted. Mix in the feta and season with salt and pepper.
3. Cut the pastry sheets into circles, fill with the spinach mixture, and fold to seal.
4. Brush with olive oil and place in the air fryer basket.
5. Air fry for 12-15 minutes until golden and crispy. Serve warm!

Nutritional Info: Calories: 250 | Fat: 14g | Carbs: 25g | Protein: 7g

CHAPTER 6: KIDFRIENDLY FAVOURITES

VEGGIE NUGGETS

Prep: 10 mins | **Cook:** 12 mins | **Serves:** 4
Cooking Function: Air Fry

Ingredients:

UK: 200g mixed vegetables (finely chopped), 100g breadcrumbs, 50g grated cheese, 1 egg, 1 teaspoon garlic powder, salt, pepper, oil spray.

US: 7oz mixed vegetables (finely chopped), 3.5oz breadcrumbs, 1.75oz grated cheese, 1 egg, 1 teaspoon garlic powder, salt, pepper, oil spray.

Instructions:

1. In a bowl, mix the chopped vegetables, breadcrumbs, cheese, egg, garlic powder, salt, and pepper until well combined.
2. Shape the mixture into small nugget shapes.
3. Preheat your air fryer to 200°C (392°F). Lightly spray the basket with oil.
4. Place the nuggets in the basket, ensuring they don't touch.
5. Cook for 1012 minutes, flipping halfway through, until golden and crispy.
6. Serve hot with your favourite dipping sauce!

Nutritional Info: Calories: 150 | Fat: 5g | Carbs: 18g | Protein: 7g

MAC AND CHEESE BITES

Prep: 15 mins | **Cook:** 8 mins | **Serves:** 4
Cooking Function: Air Fry

Ingredients:

UK: 200g macaroni (cooked), 100g cheese (grated), 50g breadcrumbs, 1 egg, salt, pepper, oil spray.

US: 7oz macaroni (cooked), 3.5oz cheese (grated), 1.75oz breadcrumbs, 1 egg, salt, pepper, oil spray.

Instructions:

1. In a bowl, combine the cooked macaroni, cheese, breadcrumbs, egg, salt, and pepper.
2. Mix until well combined and shape into small balls.
3. Preheat the air fryer to 200°C (392°F). Spray the basket with oil.
4. Arrange the mac and cheese bites in the basket.
5. Cook for 8 minutes until golden brown.
6. Enjoy them warm as a cheesy snack!

Nutritional Info: Calories: 180 | Fat: 8g | Carbs: 22g | Protein: 6g

PIZZA ROLLS

Prep: 10 mins | **Cook:** 10 mins | **Serves:** 4
Cooking Function: Air Fry

Ingredients:

UK: 200g pizza dough, 100g pizza sauce, 100g cheese (grated), 50g pepperoni (sliced), oil spray.

US: 7oz pizza dough, 3.5oz pizza sauce, 3.5oz cheese (grated), 1.75oz pepperoni (sliced), oil spray.

Instructions:

1. Roll out the pizza dough and cut it into squares.
2. Place a spoonful of pizza sauce, cheese, and pepperoni in the centre of each square.
3. Fold the dough over and seal the edges with a fork.
4. Preheat the air fryer to 200°C (392°F) and spray the basket with oil.
5. Arrange the pizza rolls in the basket and spray the tops lightly.
6. Cook for 10 minutes, flipping halfway, until golden and crispy.
7. Serve warm with extra sauce for dipping!

Nutritional Info: Calories: 220 | Fat: 9g | Carbs: 27g | Protein: 10g

SWEET POTATO FRIES

Prep: 10 mins | **Cook:** 15 mins | **Serves:** 4
Cooking Function: Air Fry

Ingredients:

UK: 500g sweet potatoes (peeled and cut into fries), 30ml olive oil, 1 teaspoon paprika, salt, pepper.

US: 17.5oz sweet potatoes (peeled and cut into fries), 2 tablespoons olive oil, 1 teaspoon paprika, salt, pepper.

Instructions:

1. In a bowl, toss the sweet potato fries with olive oil, paprika, salt, and pepper until well coated.
2. Preheat the air fryer to 200°C (392°F).
3. Arrange the fries in the basket in a single layer.
4. Cook for 1215 minutes, shaking the basket halfway through for even cooking.
5. Enjoy these crispy fries hot with your favourite dip!

Nutritional Info: Calories: 180 | Fat: 7g | Carbs: 30g | Protein: 3g

CRISPY CUCUMBER COINS

Prep: 5 mins | **Cook:** 10 mins | **Serves:** 4
Cooking Function: Air Fry

Ingredients:

UK: 2 cucumbers (sliced into coins), 30g breadcrumbs, 30g grated cheese, 1 egg, salt, pepper, oil spray.

US: 2 cucumbers (sliced into coins), 1oz breadcrumbs, 1oz grated cheese, 1 egg, salt, pepper, oil spray.

Instructions:

1. In a bowl, dip cucumber slices in beaten egg, then coat with breadcrumbs and cheese, seasoning with salt and pepper.
2. Preheat the air fryer to 200°C (392°F) and spray the basket with oil.
3. Arrange the coated cucumber coins in the basket without overlapping.
4. Cook for 8-10 minutes until crispy.
5. Serve hot with ranch dressing or any dip of your choice!

Nutritional Info: Calories: 100 | Fat: 5g | Carbs: 12g | Protein: 4g

CHEESY BROCCOLI TOTS

Prep: 10 mins | **Cook:** 15 mins | **Serves:** 4
Cooking Function: Air Fry

Ingredients:

UK: 200g broccoli (cooked and chopped), 50g cheese (grated), 50g breadcrumbs, 1 egg, salt, pepper, oil spray.

US: 7oz broccoli (cooked and chopped), 1.75oz cheese (grated), 1.75oz breadcrumbs, 1 egg, salt, pepper, oil spray.

Instructions:

1. In a bowl, mix the chopped broccoli, cheese, breadcrumbs, egg, salt, and pepper.
2. Shape the mixture into small tots.
3. Preheat your air fryer to 200°C (392°F) and spray the basket with oil.
4. Place the broccoli tots in the basket and spray the tops lightly.
5. Cook for 12-15 minutes, flipping halfway, until golden and crispy.
6. Serve warm with your favourite dipping sauce!

Nutritional Info: Calories: 130 | Fat: 6g | Carbs: 15g | Protein: 5g

RAINBOW VEGETABLE SKEWERS

Prep: 15 mins | Cook: 10 mins | Serves: 4
Cooking Function: Air Fry

Ingredients:

UK: 200g mixed bell peppers (cubed), 200g zucchini (sliced), 100g cherry tomatoes, 100g mushrooms, 30ml olive oil, salt, and pepper.

US: 7oz mixed bell peppers (cubed), 7oz zucchini (sliced), 3.5oz cherry tomatoes, 3.5oz mushrooms, 2 tablespoons olive oil, salt, pepper.

Instructions:

1. In a bowl, toss the vegetables with olive oil, salt, and pepper.
2. Thread the vegetables onto skewers.
3. Preheat the air fryer to 200°C (392°F).
4. Arrange the skewers in the basket without overcrowding.
5. Cook for 810 minutes, turning halfway through, until veggies are tender.
6. Serve warm as a colourful side or snack!

Nutritional Info: Calories: 100 | Fat: 5g | Carbs: 12g | Protein: 3g

CORN DOGS

Prep: 20 mins | Cook: 12 mins | Serves: 4
Cooking Function: Air Fry

Ingredients:

UK: 200g cornmeal, 100g all-purpose flour, 50g sugar, 1 teaspoon baking powder, 1 egg, 250ml milk, 8 vegetarian sausages, oil spray.

US: 7oz cornmeal, 3.5oz allpurpose flour, 1.75oz sugar, 1 teaspoon baking powder, 1 egg, 1 cup milk, 8 vegetarian sausages, oil spray.

Instructions:

1. In a bowl, whisk together cornmeal, flour, sugar, baking powder, egg, and milk to form a batter.
2. Dip each vegetarian sausage into the batter to coat well.
3. Preheat the air fryer to 200°C (392°F) and spray the basket with oil.
4. Place the corn-dipped sausages in the basket without overlapping.
5. Cook for 1012 minutes until golden and crispy.
6. Serve with mustard or ketchup for dipping!

Nutritional Info: Calories: 250 | Fat: 10g | Carbs: 30g | Protein: 8g

ALPHABET POTATO SHAPES

Prep: 10 mins | **Cook:** 15 mins | **Serves:** 4
Cooking Function: Air Fry
Ingredients:
UK: 500g potatoes (peeled and cut into shapes), 30ml olive oil, salt, pepper, paprika.
US: 17.5oz potatoes (peeled and cut into shapes), 2 tablespoons olive oil, salt, pepper, paprika.
Instructions:
1. Toss the potato shapes in olive oil, salt, pepper, and paprika until well coated.
2. Preheat the air fryer to 200°C (392°F).
3. Arrange the potatoes in the basket in a single layer.
4. Cook for 1215 minutes, shaking halfway, until crispy and golden.
5. Enjoy these fun shapes hot with your favourite dip!
Nutritional Info: Calories: 180 | Fat: 7g | Carbs: 25g | Protein: 3g

VEGGIELOADED TATER TOTS

Prep: 15 mins | **Cook:** 12 mins | **Serves:** 4
Cooking Function: Air Fry
Ingredients:
UK: 400g frozen tater tots, 100g mixed vegetables (chopped), 30g cheese (grated), oil spray.
US: 14oz frozen tater tots, 3.5oz mixed vegetables (chopped), 1oz cheese (grated), oil spray.
Instructions:
1. Toss the frozen tater tots with mixed vegetables and cheese.
2. Preheat the air fryer to 200°C (392°F) and spray the basket with oil.
3. Place the tater tots in the basket in a single layer.
4. Cook for 12 minutes, shaking the basket halfway for even cooking.
5. Serve hot as a cheesy, veggie-packed treat!
Nutritional Info: Calories: 220 | Fat: 10g | Carbs: 28g | Protein: 5g

CRISPY AVOCADO FRIES

Prep: 10 mins | **Cook:** 8 mins | **Serves:** 4

Cooking Function: Air Fry

Ingredients:

UK: 2 ripe avocados (sliced), 50g breadcrumbs, 30g flour, 1 egg (beaten), salt, pepper, oil spray.

US: 2 ripe avocados (sliced), 1.75oz breadcrumbs, 1oz flour, 1 egg (beaten), salt, pepper, oil spray.

Instructions:

1. Dip each avocado slice in flour, then in the beaten egg, and finally coat with breadcrumbs seasoned with salt and pepper.
2. Preheat the air fryer to 200°C (392°F) and spray the basket with oil.
3. Place the avocado fries in the basket, making sure they don't touch.
4. Cook for 68 minutes until golden and crispy.
5. Serve warm with a lime dipping sauce for a delicious snack!

Nutritional Info: Calories: 150 | Fat: 10g | Carbs: 15g | Protein: 3g

HIDDEN VEGETABLE PASTA BAKE

Prep: 15 mins | **Cook:** 25 mins | **Serves:** 4

Cooking Function: Air Fry

Ingredients:

UK: 250g pasta (cooked), 200g passata, 100g cheese (grated), 100g mixed vegetables (finely chopped), 1 teaspoon Italian herbs, salt, and pepper.

US: 8.8oz pasta (cooked), 7oz passata, 3.5oz cheese (grated), 3.5oz mixed vegetables (finely chopped), 1 teaspoon Italian herbs, salt, pepper.

Instructions:

1. In a bowl, mix the cooked pasta, passata, cheese, chopped vegetables, herbs, salt, and pepper until well combined.
2. Transfer the mixture to a suitable baking dish that fits in your air fryer.
3. Preheat the air fryer to 200°C (392°F).
4. Bake in the air fryer for 20-25 minutes until bubbly and golden on top.
5. Serve hot for a comforting meal the kids will love!

Nutritional Info: Calories: 320 | Fat: 12g | Carbs: 42g | Protein: 12g

FRUIT AND OAT COOKIES

Prep: 10 mins | **Cook:** 10 mins | **Serves:** 12

Cooking Function: Air Fry

Ingredients:

UK: 150g oats, 100g flour, 50g honey, 50g dried fruit (chopped), 1 egg, 1 teaspoon cinnamon, salt.

US: 5.3oz oats, 3.5oz flour, 1.75oz honey, 1.75oz dried fruit (chopped), 1 egg, 1 teaspoon cinnamon, salt.

Instructions:

1. In a bowl, mix the oats, flour, honey, dried fruit, egg, cinnamon, and salt until combined.
2. Preheat the air fryer to 180°C (356°F).
3. Scoop tablespoons of the mixture onto the air fryer basket, spacing them apart.
4. Cook for 8-10 minutes until golden and firm.
5. Let them cool slightly before serving as a healthy snack!

Nutritional Info: Calories: 100 | Fat: 3g | Carbs: 15g | Protein: 2g

CHAPTER 7: PARTY FOOD & SHARING PLATES

PARTY MIX SNACK MEDLEY

Prep: 10 mins | **Cook:** 10 mins | **Serves:** 6
Cooking Function: Air Fry
Ingredients:
UK: 200g mixed nuts, 100g pretzels, 100g popcorn, 30ml olive oil, 1 teaspoon smoked paprika, 1 teaspoon garlic powder, salt to taste
US: 7oz mixed nuts, 3.5oz pretzels, 3.5oz popcorn, 1oz olive oil, 1 teaspoon smoked paprika, 1 teaspoon garlic powder, salt to taste
Instructions:
1. In a large bowl, combine the mixed nuts, pretzels, and popcorn.
2. Drizzle with olive oil and sprinkle with smoked paprika, garlic powder, and salt. Toss until everything is evenly coated.
3. Preheat the air fryer to 180°C (356°F).
4. Place the mixture in the air fryer basket in a single layer.
5. Cook for 810 minutes, shaking halfway through, until golden and fragrant.
6. Serve warm in a bowl as a delightful snack to share!
Nutritional Info: Calories: 150 | Fat: 10g | Carbs: 15g | Protein: 4g

LOADED NACHOS

Prep: 15 mins | **Cook:** 10 mins | **Serves:** 4
Cooking Function: Air Fry
Ingredients:
UK: 200g tortilla chips, 100g cheese (grated), 100g black beans (drained and rinsed), 50g jalapeños (sliced), 50g salsa, 30g sour cream (for serving)
US: 7oz tortilla chips, 3.5oz cheese (grated), 3.5oz black beans (drained and rinsed), 1.75oz jalapeños (sliced), 1.75oz salsa, 1oz sour cream (for serving)

Instructions:

1. Layer half of the tortilla chips in the air fryer basket.
2. Top with half of the cheese, black beans, and jalapeños.
3. Repeat the layers with the remaining ingredients.
4. Preheat the air fryer to 200°C (392°F).
5. Cook for 8-10 minutes until the cheese is melted and bubbly.
6. Serve immediately with salsa and sour cream for dipping!

Nutritional Info: Calories: 350 | Fat: 20g | Carbs: 35g | Protein: 10g

BUFFALO CAULIFLOWER SLIDERS

Prep: 20 mins | **Cook:** 15 mins | **Serves:** 4

Cooking Function: Air Fry

Ingredients:

UK: 300g cauliflower (cut into florets), 50g buffalo sauce, 30g flour, 1 teaspoon garlic powder, 1 teaspoon onion powder, salt, pepper, slider buns (to serve)

US: 10.5oz cauliflower (cut into florets), 1.75oz buffalo sauce, 1oz flour, 1 teaspoon garlic powder, 1 teaspoon onion powder, salt, pepper, slider buns (to serve)

Instructions:

1. In a bowl, toss the cauliflower florets with flour, garlic powder, onion powder, salt, and pepper until well coated.
2. Drizzle with buffalo sauce and mix until evenly coated.
3. Preheat the air fryer to 200°C (392°F).
4. Place the cauliflower in the air fryer basket in a single layer.
5. Cook for 12-15 minutes, shaking halfway through, until crispy.
6. Serve on slider buns with your favourite toppings!

Nutritional Info: Calories: 220 | Fat: 5g | Carbs: 30g | Protein: 5g

CRISPY WONTONS

Prep: 15 mins | **Cook:** 10 mins | **Serves:** 4

Cooking Function: Air Fry

Ingredients:

UK: 200g wonton wrappers, 100g cream cheese (softened), 50g spinach (chopped), 1 teaspoon garlic powder, salt, oil spray

US: 7oz wonton wrappers, 3.5oz cream cheese (softened), 1.75oz spinach (chopped), 1 teaspoon garlic powder, salt, oil spray

Instructions:

1. In a bowl, mix the cream cheese, spinach, garlic powder, and salt until well combined.
2. Place a spoonful of the mixture in the centre of each wonton wrapper and fold to seal.
3. Preheat the air fryer to 180°C (356°F).
4. Spray the wontons lightly with oil and arrange in the air fryer basket.
5. Cook for 8-10 minutes until golden and crispy.
6. Serve hot with soy sauce or your choice of dipping sauce!

Nutritional Info: Calories: 150 | Fat: 9g | Carbs: 15g | Protein: 5g

VEGETABLE ANTIPASTO PLATTER

Prep: 10 mins | **Cook:** 10 mins | **Serves:** 4

Cooking Function: Air Fry

Ingredients:

UK: 100g cherry tomatoes, 100g bell peppers (sliced), 100g zucchini (sliced), 30ml olive oil, 1 teaspoon Italian herbs, salt, pepper

US: 3.5oz cherry tomatoes, 3.5oz bell peppers (sliced), 3.5oz zucchini (sliced), 1oz olive oil, 1 teaspoon Italian herbs, salt, pepper

Instructions:

1. In a bowl, toss the cherry tomatoes, bell peppers, and zucchini with olive oil, herbs, salt, and pepper.
2. Preheat the air fryer to 200°C (392°F).
3. Arrange the vegetables in the air fryer basket in a single layer.
4. Cook for 8-10 minutes until tender and slightly charred.
5. Serve on a platter with olives and cheese for a delightful sharing experience!

Nutritional Info: Calories: 120 | Fat: 8g | Carbs: 14g | Protein: 3g

SEVEN LAYER DIP CUPS

Prep: 15 mins | **Cook:** 0 mins | **Serves:** 6
Cooking Function: No Cook

Ingredients:

UK: 100g refried beans, 100g guacamole, 100g sour cream, 50g salsa, 50g cheese (grated), 50g chopped olives, chopped green onions (for garnish)

US: 3.5oz refried beans, 3.5oz guacamole, 3.5oz sour cream, 1.75oz salsa, 1.75oz cheese (grated), 1.75oz chopped olives, chopped green onions (for garnish)

Instructions:

1. In small cups, layer the refried beans, guacamole, sour cream, salsa, and cheese.
2. Top with chopped olives and green onions for garnish.
3. Chill in the fridge for 10-15 minutes to let the flavours meld.
4. Serve cold with tortilla chips for a fun and easy appetizer!

Nutritional Info: Calories: 180 | Fat: 12g | Carbs: 15g | Protein: 5g

MINI CALZONES

Prep: 20 mins | **Cook:** 12 mins | **Serves:** 4
Cooking Function: Air Fry

Ingredients:

UK: 250g pizza dough, 100g mozzarella (grated), 50g ricotta, 50g spinach (chopped), 1 teaspoon Italian herbs, 1 egg (for brushing)

US: 8.8oz pizza dough, 3.5oz mozzarella (grated), 1.75oz ricotta, 1.75oz spinach (chopped), 1 teaspoon Italian herbs, 1 egg (for brushing)

Instructions:

1. Roll out the pizza dough and cut it into circles.
2. In a bowl, mix the mozzarella, ricotta, spinach, and herbs.
3. Place a spoonful of the filling in the centre of each dough circle and fold over to seal.
4. Preheat the air fryer to 200°C (392°F).
5. Brush the tops with beaten eggs and arrange in the basket.
6. Cook for 10-12 minutes until golden and puffed.
7. Serve warm with marinara sauce for dipping!

Nutritional Info: Calories: 250 | Fat: 10g | Carbs: 28g | Protein: 12g

STUFFED MUSHROOM CAPS

Prep: 15 mins | **Cook:** 10 mins | **Serves:** 4
Cooking Function: Air Fry
Ingredients:

UK: 300g large mushrooms (stems removed), 100g cream cheese, 50g breadcrumbs, 30g grated cheese, 1 teaspoon garlic powder, salt, pepper

US: 10.5oz large mushrooms (stems removed), 3.5oz cream cheese, 1.75oz breadcrumbs, 1oz grated cheese, 1 teaspoon garlic powder, salt, pepper

Instructions:
1. mix the cream cheese, breadcrumbs, cheese, garlic powder, salt, and pepper until combined.
2. Stuff each mushroom cap with the filling.
3. Preheat the air fryer to 180°C (356°F).
4. Arrange the stuffed mushrooms in the air fryer basket.
5. Cook for 810 minutes until golden and bubbly.
6. Serve hot as a delicious bite-sized appetizer!

Nutritional Info: Calories: 120 | Fat: 8g | Carbs: 10g | Protein: 4g

CRISPY BRUSCHETTA BITES

Prep: 15 mins | **Cook:** 10 mins | **Serves:** 6
Cooking Function: Air Fry
Ingredients:

UK: 1 French baguette (sliced), 200g tomatoes (diced), 30ml olive oil, 1 clove garlic (minced), 1 teaspoon balsamic vinegar, salt, basil leaves (for garnish)

US: 1 French baguette (sliced), 7oz tomatoes (diced), 1oz olive oil, 1 clove garlic (minced), 1 teaspoon balsamic vinegar, salt, basil leaves (for garnish)

Instructions:
1. In a bowl, mix the diced tomatoes, olive oil, garlic, balsamic vinegar, and salt.
2. Preheat the air fryer to 200°C (392°F).
3. Arrange the baguette slices in the air fryer basket.
4. Cook for 5 minutes until crispy.
5. Top each slice with the tomato mixture and garnish with basil.
6. Serve immediately as a refreshing starter!

Nutritional Info: Calories: 180 | Fat: 5g | Carbs: 30g | Protein: 6g

VEGETABLE SPRING ROLL PLATTER

Prep: 20 mins | **Cook:** 10 mins | **Serves:** 4

Cooking Function: Air Fry

Ingredients:

UK: 10 spring roll wrappers, 150g mixed vegetables (carrots, cabbage, bell pepper), 1 teaspoon soy sauce, oil spray

US: 10 spring roll wrappers, 5.5oz mixed vegetables (carrots, cabbage, bell pepper), 1 teaspoon soy sauce, oil spray

Instructions:

1. In a bowl, mix the mixed vegetables with soy sauce.
2. Place a spoonful of the mixture in the centre of each spring roll wrapper and roll tightly.
3. Preheat the air fryer to 200°C (392°F).
4. Spray the spring rolls lightly with oil and arrange in the basket.
5. Cook for 8-10 minutes until golden and crispy.
6. Serve hot with sweet chilli sauce for dipping!

Nutritional Info: Calories: 160 | Fat: 5g | Carbs: 25g | Protein: 3g

CHEESE AND HERB BREADSTICKS

Prep: 15 mins | **Cook:** 10 mins | **Serves:** 6

Cooking Function: Air Fry

Ingredients:

UK: 250g pizza dough, 50g grated cheese, 1 teaspoon dried herbs (oregano or basil), 1 egg (for brushing)

US: 8.8oz pizza dough, 1.75oz grated cheese, 1 teaspoon dried herbs (oregano or basil), 1 egg (for brushing)

Instructions:

1. Roll out the pizza dough and cut it into strips.
2. Sprinkle with grated cheese and herbs, then twist to shape.
3. Preheat the air fryer to 200°C (392°F).
4. Brush with beaten egg and place in the air fryer basket.
5. Cook for 8-10 minutes until golden and crispy.
6. Serve warm as a cheesy snack!

Nutritional Info: Calories: 220 | Fat: 10g | Carbs: 30g | Protein: 6g

PARTY PINWHEELS

Prep: 15 mins | **Cook:** 0 mins | **Serves:** 4

Cooking Function: No Cook

Ingredients:

UK: 4 large tortillas, 100g cream cheese, 100g sliced deli vegetables (cucumber, bell pepper, carrots), 50g spinach, salt, pepper

US: 4 large tortillas, 3.5oz cream cheese, 3.5oz sliced deli vegetables (cucumber, bell pepper, carrots), 1.75oz spinach, salt, pepper

Instructions:

1. Spread cream cheese evenly over each tortilla.
2. Layer with sliced vegetables and spinach, and sprinkle with salt and pepper.
3. Roll tightly into a log and slice into pinwheels.
4. Arrange on a platter and serve as a fresh and colourful appetizer!

Nutritional Info: Calories: 150 | Fat: 6g | Carbs: 20g | Protein: 5g

SWEET POTATO TOAST CANAPÉS

Prep: 15 mins | **Cook:** 20 mins | **Serves:** 4

Cooking Function: Air Fry

Ingredients:

UK: 2 medium sweet potatoes (sliced into 1cm rounds), 100g avocado (sliced), 50g feta cheese (crumbled), 30ml olive oil, salt, pepper

US: 2 medium sweet potatoes (sliced into 0.4 rounds), 3.5oz avocado (sliced), 1.75oz feta cheese (crumbled), 1oz olive oil, salt, pepper

Instructions:

1. Preheat the air fryer to 200°C (392°F).
2. Toss the sweet potato slices in olive oil, salt, and pepper.
3. Arrange in the air fryer basket and cook for 15-20 minutes until tender and crispy.
4. Top each slice with avocado and feta before serving as a delightful canapés!

Nutritional Info: Calories: 200 | Fat: 10g | Carbs: 30g | Protein: 4g

CHAPTER 8: SIDES & ACCOMPANIMENTS

GARLIC HERB ROASTED POTATOES

Prep: 10 mins | **Cook:** 20 mins | **Serves:** 4
Cooking Function: Air Fry

Ingredients:

UK: 500g baby potatoes (halved), 30ml olive oil, 1 teaspoon dried rosemary, 1 teaspoon dried thyme, 2 cloves garlic (minced), salt, pepper

US: 17.5oz baby potatoes (halved), 1oz olive oil, 1 teaspoon dried rosemary, 1 teaspoon dried thyme, 2 cloves garlic (minced), salt, pepper

Instructions:

1. Preheat the air fryer to 200°C (392°F).
2. In a bowl, toss the halved potatoes with olive oil, rosemary, thyme, garlic, salt, and pepper until evenly coated.
3. Place the potatoes in the air fryer basket in a single layer.
4. Air fry for 1820 minutes, shaking the basket halfway through until the potatoes are crispy and golden brown.
5. Remove and serve hot as a delicious side dish to complement any main. Enjoy!

Nutritional Info: Calories: 180 | Fat: 8g | Carbs: 25g | Protein: 3g

CRISPY POLENTA CHIPS

Prep: 5 mins | **Cook:** 15 mins | **Serves:** 4
Cooking Function: Air Fry

Ingredients:

UK: 250g readymade polenta (sliced into chips), 20ml olive oil, 1 teaspoon paprika, ½ teaspoon garlic powder, salt, pepper

US: 8.8oz readymade polenta (sliced into chips), 0.7oz olive oil, 1 teaspoon paprika, ½ teaspoon garlic powder, salt, pepper

Instructions:

1. Preheat the air fryer to 200°C (392°F).
2. Toss the polenta chips in olive oil, paprika, garlic powder, salt, and pepper.
3. Place the polenta chips in the air fryer basket in a single layer.
4. Air fry for 1215 minutes, flipping halfway through, until crispy and golden.
5. Serve with your favourite dipping sauce as a crunchy side or snack.

Nutritional Info: Calories: 130 | Fat: 5g | Carbs: 18g | Protein: 2g

MEDITERRANEAN ROASTED VEGETABLES

Prep: 10 mins | **Cook:** 15 mins | **Serves:** 4
Cooking Function: Air Fry
Ingredients:
UK: 1 red pepper (sliced), 1 yellow pepper (sliced), 1 courgette (sliced), 1 red onion (quartered), 30ml olive oil, 1 teaspoon dried oregano, salt, pepper
US: 1 red pepper (sliced), 1 yellow pepper (sliced), 1 zucchini (sliced), 1 red onion (quartered), 1oz olive oil, 1 teaspoon dried oregano, salt, pepper
Instructions:
1. Preheat the air fryer to 180°C (356°F).
2. In a large bowl, toss the sliced vegetables with olive oil, oregano, salt, and pepper.
3. Spread the vegetables in the air fryer basket in a single layer.
4. Air fry for 1215 minutes, shaking the basket occasionally, until tender and slightly charred.
5. Serve as a colourful, flavour-packed side dish.
Nutritional Info: Calories: 95 | Fat: 7g | Carbs: 8g | Protein: 1g

CAULIFLOWER RICE

Prep: 5 mins | **Cook:** 10 mins | **Serves:** 4
Cooking Function: Air Fry
Ingredients:
UK: 1 medium cauliflower (cut into florets), 15ml olive oil, 1 teaspoon cumin, salt, pepper
US: 1 medium cauliflower (cut into florets), 0.5oz olive oil, 1 teaspoon cumin, salt, pepper
Instructions:
1. Preheat the air fryer to 180°C (356°F).
2. Pulse the cauliflower florets in a food processor until they resemble rice.
3. Toss the cauliflower rice with olive oil, cumin, salt, and pepper.
4. Spread the cauliflower rice evenly in the air fryer basket.
5. Air fry for 810 minutes, stirring halfway through, until lightly browned and tender.
6. Serve as a low-carb side to your favourite mains.
Nutritional Info: Calories: 70 | Fat: 4g | Carbs: 6g | Protein: 2g

CRISPY QUINOA

Prep: 5 mins | **Cook:** 15 mins | **Serves:** 4
Cooking Function: Air Fry
Ingredients:
UK: 200g cooked quinoa, 15ml olive oil, 1 teaspoon paprika, salt, pepper
US: 7oz cooked quinoa, 0.5oz olive oil, 1 teaspoon paprika, salt, pepper
Instructions:
1. Preheat the air fryer to 200°C (392°F).
2. Toss the cooked quinoa with olive oil, paprika, salt, and pepper.
3. Spread the quinoa in a thin layer in the air fryer basket.
4. Air fry for 12-15 minutes, stirring occasionally, until crispy.
5. Sprinkle over salads or serve as a crunchy side dish.
Nutritional Info: Calories: 120 | Fat: 5g | Carbs: 16g | Protein: 4g

STUFFED BABY POTATOES

Prep: 10 mins | **Cook:** 20 mins | **Serves:** 4
Cooking Function: Air Fry
Ingredients:
UK: 500g baby potatoes, 50g cream cheese, 30g cheddar cheese (grated), 2 spring onions (chopped), salt, pepper
US: 17.5oz baby potatoes, 1.75oz cream cheese, 1oz cheddar cheese (grated), 2 green onions (chopped), salt, pepper
Instructions:
1. Preheat the air fryer to 200°C (392°F).
2. Pierce the baby potatoes with a fork and place them in the air fryer. Cook for 15-18 minutes until tender.
3. Cut a small slit in each potato and scoop out some of the flesh.
4. In a bowl, mix the potato flesh with cream cheese, cheddar, spring onions, salt, and pepper.
5. Spoon the mixture back into the potatoes and air fry for an additional 5 minutes until the tops are golden and crispy.
6. Serve hot as a perfect bite-sized snack or side dish.
Nutritional Info: Calories: 190 | Fat: 8g | Carbs: 25g | Protein: 5g

HERBED DINNER ROLLS

Prep: 15 mins | **Cook:** 10 mins | **Serves:** 6 rolls
Cooking Function: Bake

Ingredients:

UK: 300g plain flour, 1 teaspoon dried thyme, 1 teaspoon dried oregano, 7g instant yeast, 150ml warm water, 30ml olive oil, salt

US: 10.5oz plain flour, 1 teaspoon dried thyme, 1 teaspoon dried oregano, 0.25oz instant yeast, 5oz warm water, 1oz olive oil, salt

Instructions:

1. Preheat the air fryer to 180°C (356°F).
2. In a large bowl, mix the flour, dried herbs, yeast, and a pinch of salt. Slowly add the warm water and olive oil, mixing until a dough forms.
3. Knead the dough for about 5 minutes until smooth and elastic. Divide into 6 small rolls.
4. Place the rolls in the air fryer and bake for 8-10 minutes until golden and cooked through.
5. Serve warm, perfect with soups or as a side to any meal.

Nutritional Info: Calories: 160 | Fat: 4g | Carbs: 27g | Protein: 4g

CRISPY ONION STRINGS

Prep: 10 mins | **Cook:** 10 mins | **Serves:** 4
Cooking Function: Air Fry

Ingredients:

UK: 2 medium onions (thinly sliced), 100g plain flour, 1 teaspoon paprika, 1 teaspoon garlic powder, 30ml olive oil, salt, pepper

US: 2 medium onions (thinly sliced), 3.5oz plain flour, 1 teaspoon paprika, 1 teaspoon garlic powder, 1oz olive oil, salt, pepper

Instructions:

1. Preheat the air fryer to 200°C (392°F).
2. In a bowl, toss the onion slices with flour, paprika, garlic powder, salt, and pepper.
3. Drizzle olive oil over the coated onions and toss to ensure they're evenly coated.
4. Spread the onion slices in the air fryer basket and air fry for 8-10 minutes, shaking the basket halfway through, until golden and crispy.
5. Serve as a crunchy side or as a topping for burgers and salads.

Nutritional Info: Calories: 130 | Fat: 6g | Carbs: 18g | Protein: 2g

ROASTED CHERRY TOMATOES

Prep: 5 mins | **Cook:** 10 mins | **Serves:** 4
Cooking Function: Air Fry
Ingredients:
UK: 300g cherry tomatoes, 15ml olive oil, 1 teaspoon balsamic vinegar, salt, pepper, fresh basil (for garnish)
US: 10.5oz cherry tomatoes, 0.5oz olive oil, 1 teaspoon balsamic vinegar, salt, pepper, fresh basil (for garnish)
Instructions:
1. Preheat the air fryer to 180°C (356°F).
2. Toss the cherry tomatoes in olive oil, balsamic vinegar, salt, and pepper.
3. Place the tomatoes in the air fryer basket and roast for 8-10 minutes, shaking halfway through, until they start to burst and caramelise.
4. Garnish with fresh basil before serving as a vibrant side dish or topping for salads and pasta.
Nutritional Info: Calories: 60 | Fat: 4g | Carbs: 6g | Protein: 1g

GREEN BEAN ALMONDINE

Prep: 5 mins | **Cook:** 8 mins | **Serves:** 4
Cooking Function: Air Fry
Ingredients:
UK: 300g green beans (trimmed), 30g flaked almonds, 15ml olive oil, 1 clove garlic (minced), salt, pepper
US: 10.5oz green beans (trimmed), 1oz flaked almonds, 0.5oz olive oil, 1 clove garlic (minced), salt, pepper
Instructions:
1. Preheat the air fryer to 190°C (374°F).
2. Toss the green beans in olive oil, garlic, salt, and pepper.
3. Spread the green beans in a single layer in the air fryer basket and cook for 6-8 minutes, shaking the basket halfway through.
4. Add the flaked almonds in the last 2 minutes of cooking to toast.
5. Serve as a deliciously nutty side dish perfect for any meal.
Nutritional Info: Calories: 90 | Fat: 7g | Carbs: 5g | Protein: 2g

CRISPY ROASTED CHICKPEAS

Prep: 5 mins | **Cook:** 15 mins | **Serves:** 4

Cooking Function: Air Fry

Ingredients:

UK: 400g tin chickpeas (drained and rinsed), 15ml olive oil, 1 teaspoon paprika, ½ teaspoon garlic powder, salt

US: 14oz tin chickpeas (drained and rinsed), 0.5oz olive oil, 1 teaspoon paprika, ½ teaspoon garlic powder, salt

Instructions:

1. Preheat the air fryer to 200°C (392°F).
2. Pat the chickpeas dry with a kitchen towel. Toss them in olive oil, paprika, garlic powder, and a pinch of salt.
3. Spread the chickpeas in the air fryer basket in a single layer and cook for 12-15 minutes, shaking the basket occasionally, until crispy.
4. Serve as a crunchy snack or salad topping.

Nutritional Info: Calories: 110 | Fat: 5g | Carbs: 13g | Protein: 4g

PARMESAN ZUCCHINI ROUNDS

Prep: 5 mins | Cook: 10 mins | Serves: 4

Cooking Function: Air Fry

Ingredients:

UK: 2 medium courgettes (sliced into rounds), 30g grated parmesan cheese, 15ml olive oil, 1 teaspoon dried oregano, salt, pepper

US: 2 medium zucchinis (sliced into rounds), 1oz grated parmesan cheese, 0.5oz olive oil, 1 teaspoon dried oregano, salt, pepper

Instructions:

1. Preheat the air fryer to 200°C (392°F).
2. Toss the zucchini rounds in olive oil, oregano, salt, and pepper.
3. Lay the rounds in the air fryer basket and sprinkle with grated parmesan.
4. Air fry for 8-10 minutes until golden and crispy.
5. Serve as a cheesy and delicious side or snack.

Nutritional Info: Calories: 80 | Fat: 5g | Carbs: 4g | Protein: 4g

SWEET POTATO WEDGES

Prep: 5 mins | **Cook:** 15 mins | **Serves:** 4

Cooking Function: Air Fry

Ingredients:

UK: 2 large sweet potatoes (cut into wedges), 30ml olive oil, 1 teaspoon smoked paprika, ½ teaspoon garlic powder, salt, pepper

US: 2 large sweet potatoes (cut into wedges), 1oz olive oil, 1 teaspoon smoked paprika, ½ teaspoon garlic powder, salt, pepper

Instructions:

1. Preheat the air fryer to 200°C (392°F).
2. Toss the sweet potato wedges in olive oil, smoked paprika, garlic powder, salt, and pepper.
3. Spread the wedges in the air fryer basket in a single layer.
4. Air fry for 1215 minutes, shaking the basket halfway through, until golden and crispy.
5. Serve as a perfect side to any main or as a tasty snack.

Nutritional Info: Calories: 140 | Fat: 6g | Carbs: 20g | Protein: 2g

CHAPTER 9: SAUCES & DIPS

ROASTED RED PEPPER HUMMUS

Prep: 10 mins | **Cook:** 25 mins | **Serves:** 6
Cooking Function: Air Fry
Ingredients:
UK: 2 large red peppers, 400g tin chickpeas (drained and rinsed), 2 tablespoons tahini, 1 garlic clove, 30ml lemon juice, 30ml olive oil, salt, pepper
US: 2 large red bell peppers, 14oz tin chickpeas (drained and rinsed), 2 tablespoons tahini, 1 garlic clove, 2 tablespoons lemon juice, 2 tablespoons olive oil, salt, pepper
Instructions:
1. Preheat the air fryer to 200°C (392°F).
2. Place the red peppers in the air fryer basket and roast for 2025 minutes, turning halfway, until the skins are charred.
3. Once roasted, place the peppers in a bowl and cover with cling film for 10 minutes to allow the skins to loosen.
4. Peel the peppers and discard the seeds.
5. In a food processor, blend the roasted peppers, chickpeas, tahini, garlic, lemon juice, olive oil, salt, and pepper until smooth.
6. Adjust seasoning to taste and serve with pitta or veggie sticks.
Nutritional Info: Calories: 170 | Fat: 7g | Carbs: 22g | Protein: 5g

SPINACH AND ARTICHOKE DIP

Prep: 10 mins | **Cook:** 15 mins | **Serves:** 4
Cooking Function: Air Fry
Ingredients:
UK: 150g frozen spinach (thawed and drained), 150g artichoke hearts (drained and chopped), 50g cream cheese, 50g sour cream, 30g parmesan cheese (grated), 1 garlic clove (minced), salt, pepper
US: 5.5oz frozen spinach (thawed and drained), 5.5oz artichoke hearts (drained and chopped), 1.75oz cream cheese, 1.75oz sour cream, 1oz parmesan cheese (grated), 1 garlic clove (minced), salt, pepper

Instructions:

1. Preheat the air fryer to 180°C (356°F).
2. In a bowl, mix the spinach, artichoke hearts, cream cheese, sour cream, parmesan, garlic, salt, and pepper.
3. Transfer the mixture to an air fryersafe dish and cook for 1015 minutes, until bubbling and golden on top.
4. Serve warm with tortilla chips or crusty bread.

Nutritional Info: Calories: 200 | Fat: 15g | Carbs: 7g | Protein: 6g

BAKED RICOTTA

Prep: 5 mins | Cook: 20 mins | Serves: 4

Cooking Function: Bake

Ingredients:

UK: 250g ricotta cheese, 1 tablespoon honey, 1 tablespoon olive oil, 1 teaspoon lemon zest, salt, pepper

US: 8.8oz ricotta cheese, 1 tablespoon honey, 1 tablespoon olive oil, 1 teaspoon lemon zest, salt, pepper

Instructions:

1. Preheat the air fryer to 180°C (356°F).
2. In a bowl, mix the ricotta cheese, honey, lemon zest, salt, and pepper.
3. Transfer the mixture to an air fryersafe dish and drizzle with olive oil.
4. Bake for 1520 minutes until lightly golden and set.
5. Serve with toasted bread or as a spread for crackers.

Nutritional Info: Calories: 150 | Fat: 10g | Carbs: 5g | Protein: 8g

ROASTED GARLIC AIOLI

Prep: 5 mins | **Cook:** 15 mins | **Serves:** 4
Cooking Function: Air Fry
Ingredients:
UK: 1 whole garlic bulb, 60ml mayonnaise, 1 teaspoon lemon juice, salt, pepper
US: 1 whole garlic bulb, 2oz mayonnaise, 1 teaspoon lemon juice, salt, pepper
Instructions:
1. Preheat the air fryer to 180°C (356°F).
2. Cut the top off the garlic bulb, drizzle with olive oil, and wrap in foil.
3. Air fry the garlic for 1215 minutes until soft and golden.
4. Squeeze the roasted garlic cloves into a bowl and mix with mayonnaise, lemon juice, salt, and pepper.
5. Serve as a dip or spread for sandwiches and roasted veggies.
Nutritional Info: Calories: 120 | Fat: 10g | Carbs: 6g | Protein: 1g

CRISPY SEASONED OIL

Prep: 5 mins | **Cook:** 8 mins | **Serves:** 4
Cooking Function: Air Fry
Ingredients:
UK: 60ml olive oil, 1 teaspoon smoked paprika, 1 teaspoon garlic powder, 1 teaspoon dried thyme, salt, pepper
US: 2oz olive oil, 1 teaspoon smoked paprika, 1 teaspoon garlic powder, 1 teaspoon dried thyme, salt, pepper
Instructions:
1. Preheat the air fryer to 200°C (392°F).
2. In a small dish, combine the olive oil, paprika, garlic powder, thyme, salt, and pepper.
3. Air fry for 68 minutes, stirring occasionally, until the oil is fragrant and slightly crispy.
4. Drizzle over vegetables, and breads, or use as a dipping oil.
Nutritional Info: Calories: 90 | Fat: 9g | Carbs: 1g | Protein: 0g

ROMESCO SAUCE

Prep: 10 mins | **Cook:** 15 mins | **Serves:** 4
Cooking Function: Air Fry

Ingredients:

UK: 2 large red peppers, 1 slice white bread (toasted), 30g almonds, 1 garlic clove, 1 tablespoon red wine vinegar, 30ml olive oil, salt, pepper

US: 2 large red bell peppers, 1 slice white bread (toasted), 1oz almonds, 1 garlic clove, 1 tablespoon red wine vinegar, 2 tablespoons olive oil, salt, pepper

Instructions:

1. Preheat the air fryer to 200°C (392°F).
2. Roast the peppers in the air fryer for 15 minutes, turning halfway, until charred.
3. Peel the peppers and blend with the toasted bread, almonds, garlic, vinegar, olive oil, salt, and pepper until smooth.
4. Serve with grilled vegetables, as a dip, or over pasta.

Nutritional Info: Calories: 180 | Fat: 13g | Carbs: 10g | Protein: 4g

ROASTED TOMATO SALSA

Prep: 5 mins | **Cook:** 10 mins | **Serves:** 4
Cooking Function: Air Fry

Ingredients:

UK: 300g cherry tomatoes, 1 small onion (chopped), 1 jalapeño (chopped), 1 garlic clove (minced), 15ml olive oil, salt, pepper, fresh coriander

US: 10.5oz cherry tomatoes, 1 small onion (chopped), 1 jalapeño (chopped), 1 garlic clove (minced), 1 tablespoon olive oil, salt, pepper, fresh cilantro

Instructions:

1. Preheat the air fryer to 200°C (392°F).
2. Toss the cherry tomatoes, onion, jalapeño, and garlic in olive oil, salt, and pepper.
3. Air fry for 810 minutes, until the tomatoes are blistered and the onion is soft.
4. Blend briefly for a chunky salsa and stir in fresh coriander. Serve with tortilla chips.

Nutritional Info: Calories: 60 | Fat: 4g | Carbs: 6g | Protein: 1g

BABA GANOUSH

Prep: 10 mins | **Cook:** 20 mins | **Serves:** 4
Cooking Function: Air Fry
Ingredients:

UK: 1 large aubergine, 2 tablespoons tahini, 1 garlic clove, 30ml lemon juice, 15ml olive oil, salt, pepper, smoked paprika (for garnish)

US: 1 large eggplant, 2 tablespoons tahini, 1 garlic clove, 2 tablespoons lemon juice, 1 tablespoon olive oil, salt, pepper, smoked paprika (for garnish)

Instructions:

1. Preheat the air fryer to 200°C (392°F).
2. Pierce the aubergine and place it in the air fryer. Cook for 20 minutes, turning halfway, until soft and charred.
3. Scoop out the flesh and blend with tahini, garlic, lemon juice, olive oil, salt, and pepper.
4. Garnish with smoked paprika and serve with flatbread or veggies.

Nutritional Info: Calories: 120 | Fat: 8g | Carbs: 10g | Protein: 3g

CASHEW CHEESE SAUCE

Prep: 5 mins | **Cook:** 0 mins | **Serves:** 4
Cooking Function: N/A
Ingredients:

UK: 150g raw cashews (soaked), 30ml lemon juice, 1 tablespoon nutritional yeast, 1 garlic clove, 120ml water, salt, pepper

US: 5.5oz raw cashews (soaked), 2 tablespoons lemon juice, 1 tablespoon nutritional yeast, 1 garlic clove, 1/2 cup water, salt, pepper

Instructions:

1. Drain the soaked cashews and add to a blender with lemon juice, nutritional yeast, garlic, water, salt, and pepper.
2. Blend until smooth and creamy.
3. Serve as a dip for veggies, or use as a sauce for pasta or nachos.

Nutritional Info: Calories: 160 | Fat: 10g | Carbs: 12g | Protein: 5g

CRISPY CHICKPEA HUMMUS

Prep: 10 mins | **Cook:** 20 mins | **Serves:** 6
Cooking Function: Air Fry

Ingredients:

UK: 400g tin chickpeas (drained and rinsed), 2 tablespoons olive oil, 2 teaspoons smoked paprika, 1 garlic clove (minced), 2 tablespoons tahini, 30ml lemon juice, salt, pepper

US: 14oz tin chickpeas (drained and rinsed), 2 tablespoons olive oil, 2 teaspoons smoked paprika, 1 garlic clove (minced), 2 tablespoons tahini, 2 tablespoons lemon juice, salt, pepper

Instructions:

1. Preheat the air fryer to 200°C (392°F).
2. Toss the chickpeas with olive oil, paprika, and salt. Air fry for 15-20 minutes until crispy, shaking halfway.
3. Blend the crispy chickpeas with garlic, tahini, lemon juice, salt, and pepper until smooth.
4. Serve with veggie sticks or pita chips.

Nutritional Info: Calories: 180 | Fat: 8g | Carbs: 24g | Protein: 5g

ROASTED VEGETABLE PESTO

Prep: 10 mins | **Cook:** 20 mins | **Serves:** 4
Cooking Function: Roast

Ingredients:

UK: 150g mixed roasted vegetables (e.g., peppers, zucchini, eggplant), 50g fresh basil leaves, 50g pine nuts (toasted), 50g Parmesan cheese (grated), 60ml olive oil, salt and pepper (to taste)

US: 5oz mixed roasted vegetables (e.g., bell peppers, zucchini, eggplant), 2oz fresh basil leaves, 2oz pine nuts (toasted), 2oz Parmesan cheese (grated), ¼ cup olive oil, salt and pepper (to taste)

Instructions:

1. Preheat your air fryer to 200°C (390°F).
2. Roast your choice of vegetables in the air fryer for about 15-20 minutes until tender and slightly charred.
3. In a food processor, combine the roasted vegetables, basil, pine nuts, Parmesan, olive oil, salt, and pepper.
4. Blend until smooth, adjusting the oil for your desired consistency.
5. Serve over pasta, spread on bread, or as a dip.

Nutritional Info: Calories: 250 | Fat: 20g | Carbs: 15g | Protein: 6g

SWEET CHILI SAUCE

Prep: 5 mins | **Cook:** 10 mins | **Serves:** 4

Cooking Function: Air Fry

Ingredients:

UK: 100ml rice vinegar, 75g sugar, 50g sweet chilli sauce, 1 teaspoon cornstarch (mixed with 1 tablespoon water), salt (to taste)

US: ⅓ cup rice vinegar, ½ cup sugar, ¼ cup sweet chilli sauce, 1 teaspoon cornstarch (mixed with 1 tablespoon water), salt (to taste)

Instructions:

1. In a saucepan over medium heat, combine rice vinegar, sugar, and sweet chilli sauce. Stir until sugar dissolves.
2. Add the cornstarch mixture, stirring continuously until the sauce thickens.
3. Season with a pinch of salt.
4. Remove from heat and let it cool before serving as a dipping sauce or drizzle over dishes.

Nutritional Info: Calories: 120 | Fat: 0g | Carbs: 30g | Protein: 0g

SMOKY VEGAN QUESO

Prep: 10 mins | **Cook:** 10 mins | **Serves:** 4
Cooking Function: Air Fry

Ingredients:

UK: 150g cashews (soaked for 2 hours), 200ml water, 1 tablespoon nutritional yeast, 1 teaspoon smoked paprika, 1 garlic clove (minced), salt and pepper (to taste)

US: 5oz cashews (soaked for 2 hours), ¾ cup water, 1 tablespoon nutritional yeast, 1 teaspoon smoked paprika, 1 garlic clove (minced), salt and pepper (to taste)

Instructions:

1. Drain and rinse the soaked cashews.
2. In a blender, combine the cashews, water, nutritional yeast, smoked paprika, garlic, and a pinch of salt and pepper.
3. Blend until smooth and creamy, adding more water if needed for your desired consistency.
4. Taste and adjust seasoning as necessary.
5. Serve warm with tortilla chips, over nachos, or as a topping for tacos.

Nutritional Info: Calories: 210 | Fat: 18g | Carbs: 9g | Protein: 6g

CHAPTER 10: DESSERTS

APPLE CRISPS

Prep: 10 mins | **Cook:** 15 mins | **Serves:** 4
Cooking Function: Air Fry
Ingredients:
UK: 4 medium apples (cored and thinly sliced), 1 teaspoon ground cinnamon, 30g sugar, 1 tablespoon lemon juice
US: 4 medium apples (cored and thinly sliced), 1 teaspoon ground cinnamon, 2 tablespoons sugar, 1 tablespoon lemon juice
Instructions:
1. Preheat your air fryer to 160°C (320°F).
2. In a large bowl, toss the apple slices with lemon juice, sugar, and cinnamon until well coated.
3. Arrange the apple slices in a single layer in the air fryer basket, ensuring they aren't overlapping.
4. Air fry for 10-15 minutes, flipping halfway through until the apples are crispy and golden.
5. Once done, let them cool before serving as a delicious snack or dessert!

Nutritional Info: Calories: 120 | Fat: 0g | Carbs: 31g | Protein: 0g

CINNAMON SUGAR CHURROS

Prep: 15 mins | **Cook:** 10 mins | **Serves:** 4
Cooking Function: Air Fry
Ingredients:
UK: 125ml water, 50g unsalted butter, 1 tablespoon sugar, 1/2 teaspoon salt, 100g plain flour, 1 egg, 50g sugar (for coating), 1 teaspoon ground cinnamon
US: ½ cup water, 4 tablespoons unsalted butter, 1 tablespoon sugar, ½ teaspoon salt, ⅓ cup all-purpose flour, 1 egg, ¼ cup sugar (for coating), 1 teaspoon ground cinnamon

Instructions:
1. In a saucepan over medium heat, combine water, butter, sugar, and salt. Bring to a boil.
2. Remove from heat and stir in the flour until a dough forms. Allow to cool slightly before mixing in the egg until smooth.
3. Preheat your air fryer to 200°C (400°F).
4. Spoon the dough into a piping bag fitted with a star tip. Pipe strips of dough onto parchment paper.
5. Air fry for 8-10 minutes until golden brown.
6. Mix the sugar and cinnamon and toss the warm churros in the mixture before serving.

Nutritional Info: Calories: 250 | Fat: 10g | Carbs: 36g | Protein: 3g

CHOCOLATE LAVA CAKES

Prep: 10 mins | **Cook:** 12 mins | **Serves:** 2

Cooking Function: Bake

Ingredients:

UK: 100g dark chocolate (chopped), 100g unsalted butter, 2 eggs, 50g sugar, 30g plain flour, 1 teaspoon vanilla extract

US: 3.5oz dark chocolate (chopped), 3.5oz unsalted butter, 2 eggs, ¼ cup sugar, ¼ cup all-purpose flour, 1 teaspoon vanilla extract

Instructions:
1. Preheat your air fryer to 180°C (356°F).
2. Melt the chocolate and butter together in a bowl over simmering water. Stir until smooth.
3. In a separate bowl, whisk together the eggs and sugar until pale. Stir in the melted chocolate mixture and vanilla.
4. Fold in the flour gently until just combined.
5. Grease two ramekins and pour the batter in, filling them halfway.
6. Air fry for 10-12 minutes until the edges are set but the centre is still soft.
7. Allow to cool for a minute, then invert onto a plate. Serve warm with ice cream!

Nutritional Info: Calories: 300 | Fat: 20g | Carbs: 30g | Protein: 6g

BANANA FRITTERS

Prep: 10 mins | **Cook:** 12 mins | **Serves:** 4

Cooking Function: Air Fry

Ingredients:

UK: 2 ripe bananas (mashed), 100g plain flour, 50g sugar, 1 teaspoon baking powder, 1 teaspoon vanilla extract, 30ml milk

US: 2 ripe bananas (mashed), ¾ cup all-purpose flour, ¼ cup sugar, 1 teaspoon baking powder, 1 teaspoon vanilla extract, 2 tablespoons milk

Instructions:

1. Preheat your air fryer to 200°C (400°F).
2. In a bowl, mix the mashed bananas, flour, sugar, baking powder, vanilla, and milk until combined.
3. Scoop spoonfuls of the mixture onto parchment paper in the air fryer basket.
4. Air fry for 10-12 minutes until golden and crispy.
5. Allow to cool slightly before serving with honey or maple syrup.

Nutritional Info: Calories: 180 | Fat: 1g | Carbs: 38g | Protein: 3g

BERRY TURNOVERS

Prep: 15 mins | **Cook:** 15 mins | **Serves:** 4

Cooking Function: Air Fry

Ingredients:

UK: 250g puff pastry, 150g mixed berries (fresh or frozen), 30g sugar, 1 tablespoon cornflour, 1 egg (beaten for egg wash)

US: 9oz puff pastry, 1 cup mixed berries (fresh or frozen), ¼ cup sugar, 1 tablespoon cornstarch, 1 egg (beaten for egg wash)

Instructions:

1. Preheat your air fryer to 200°C (400°F).
2. Roll out the puff pastry on a floured surface and cut into squares.
3. In a bowl, mix the berries with sugar and cornflour until coated.
4. Place a spoonful of the berry mixture in the centre of each pastry square. Fold and seal edges with a fork.
5. Brush the tops with beaten egg.
6. Air fry for 12-15 minutes until golden and puffed. Serve warm!

Nutritional Info: Calories: 220 | Fat: 12g | Carbs: 25g | Protein: 3g

CRISPY PEANUT BUTTER CUPS

Prep: 15 mins | **Cook:** 5 mins | **Serves:** 6
Cooking Function: Air Fry

Ingredients:

UK: 150g dark chocolate (chopped), 100g creamy peanut butter, 30g powdered sugar, 1 teaspoon vanilla extract, 6 cupcake liners

US: 5oz dark chocolate (chopped), ½ cup creamy peanut butter, ¼ cup powdered sugar, 1 teaspoon vanilla extract, 6 cupcake liners

Instructions:

1. Preheat your air fryer to 180°C (356°F).
2. Melt the chocolate in a bowl over simmering water until smooth.
3. Line a muffin tray with cupcake liners. Pour a thin layer of melted chocolate into each liner.
4. Freeze for 5 minutes until set.
5. Mix peanut butter, powdered sugar, and vanilla until smooth. Spoon the mixture over the set chocolate.
6. Top with remaining chocolate and air fry for 5 minutes. Allow to cool before serving.

Nutritional Info: Calories: 250 | Fat: 18g | Carbs: 20g | Protein: 6g

FRUIT CRUMBLE

Prep: 10 mins | **Cook:** 25 mins | **Serves:** 4
Cooking Function: Bake

Ingredients:

UK: 400g mixed fruit (e.g., apples, berries), 100g oats, 50g flour, 50g brown sugar, 50g butter (melted), 1 teaspoon cinnamon

US: 14oz mixed fruit (e.g., apples, berries), 1 cup oats, ⅓ cup flour, ¼ cup brown sugar, ¼ cup butter (melted), 1 teaspoon cinnamon

Instructions:

1. Preheat your air fryer to 180°C (356°F).
2. In a bowl, mix the fruit with half the sugar and cinnamon. Spread it in a baking dish.
3. In another bowl, combine oats, flour, remaining sugar, and melted butter until crumbly.
4. Sprinkle the crumble topping over the fruit.
5. Bake in the air fryer for 2025 minutes until golden and bubbly. Serve warm with ice cream!

Nutritional Info: Calories: 350 | Fat: 15g | Carbs: 52g | Protein: 4g

SWEET POTATO BROWNIES

Prep: 15 mins | **Cook:** 20 mins | **Serves:** 4
Cooking Function: Bake
Ingredients:
UK: 200g sweet potatoes (mashed), 100g dark chocolate (melted), 50g sugar, 50g plain flour, 1 teaspoon vanilla extract, 1 teaspoon baking powder
US: 7oz sweet potatoes (mashed), 3.5oz dark chocolate (melted), ¼ cup sugar, ⅓ cup all-purpose flour, 1 teaspoon vanilla extract, 1 teaspoon baking powder
Instructions:
1. Preheat your air fryer to 180°C (356°F).
2. In a bowl, combine mashed sweet potatoes, melted chocolate, Sugar, flour, vanilla, and baking powder until smooth.
3. Pour the batter into a greased baking dish.
4. Bake for 1820 minutes until firm and set.
5. Allow to cool before cutting into squares. Enjoy as a healthy dessert!
Nutritional Info: Calories: 220 | Fat: 10g | Carbs: 30g | Protein: 3g

CRISPY PIE CRUST COOKIES

Prep: 10 mins | **Cook:** 8 mins | **Serves:** 8
Cooking Function: Air Fry
Ingredients:
UK: 250g pie crust pastry, 50g sugar, 1 teaspoon cinnamon, 30ml melted butter
US: 9oz pie crust pastry, ¼ cup sugar, 1 teaspoon cinnamon, 2 tablespoons melted butter
Instructions:
1. Preheat your air fryer to 200°C (400°F).
2. Roll out the pie crust on a floured surface and cut it into cookie shapes.
3. Brush each cookie with melted butter and sprinkle with sugar and cinnamon.
4. Arrange the cookies in the air fryer basket in a single layer.
5. Air fry for 68 minutes until golden and crispy. Let cool before serving.
Nutritional Info: Calories: 150 | Fat: 8g | Carbs: 20g | Protein: 2g

STUFFED BAKED APPLES

Prep: 15 mins | **Cook:** 15 mins | **Serves:** 4

Cooking Function: Bake

Ingredients:

UK: 4 medium apples (cored), 50g oats, 50g walnuts (chopped), 30g honey, 1 teaspoon cinnamon, 30ml water

US: 4 medium apples (cored), ½ cup oats, ½ cup walnuts (chopped), 2 tablespoons honey, 1 teaspoon cinnamon, 2 tablespoons water

Instructions:

1. Preheat your air fryer to 180°C (356°F).
2. In a bowl, mix oats, walnuts, honey, and cinnamon.
3. Stuff the mixture into each cored apple and place them in the air fryer basket.
4. Pour water into the basket to create steam.
5. Air fry for 12-15 minutes until apples are tender. Serve warm!

Nutritional Info: Calories: 180 | Fat: 7g | Carbs: 27g | Protein: 3g

CHOCOLATE CHIP COOKIE CUPS

Prep: 10 mins | **Cook:** 8 mins | **Serves:** 6

Cooking Function: Bake

Ingredients:

UK: 100g plain flour, 50g brown sugar, 50g butter (softened), 1 egg, 50g chocolate chips, 1 teaspoon vanilla extract

US: ⅔ cup all-purpose flour, ¼ cup brown sugar, ¼ cup butter (softened), 1 egg, ⅓ cup chocolate chips, 1 teaspoon vanilla extract

Instructions:

1. Preheat your air fryer to 180°C (356°F).
2. In a bowl, cream together the butter and brown sugar. Add the egg and vanilla, mixing well.
3. Fold in the flour and chocolate chips until combined.
4. Spoon the mixture into greased muffin cups.
5. Air fry for 6-8 minutes until the edges are golden and the centre is set. Let cool before serving.

Nutritional Info: Calories: 200 | Fat: 10g | Carbs: 25g | Protein: 3g

CRISPY RICE PUDDING BALLS

Prep: 15 mins | **Cook:** 15 mins | **Serves:** 8
Cooking Function: Air Fry

Ingredients:

UK: 250g cooked rice, 50g sugar, 1 egg, 100g breadcrumbs, 1 teaspoon cinnamon, oil spray

US: 1 cup cooked rice, ¼ cup sugar, 1 egg, ⅓ cup breadcrumbs, 1 teaspoon cinnamon, oil spray

Instructions:

1. In a bowl, combine cooked rice, sugar, egg, and cinnamon until mixed.
2. Form the mixture into small balls, then roll in breadcrumbs.
3. Preheat your air fryer to 200°C (400°F).
4. Spray the air fryer basket with oil and place the balls inside.
5. Air fry for 12-15 minutes until crispy and golden. Serve warm!

Nutritional Info: Calories: 180 | Fat: 5g | Carbs: 30g | Protein: 4g

MINI FRUIT PIES

Prep: 15 mins | **Cook:** 12 mins | **Serves:** 6
Cooking Function: Bake

Ingredients:

UK: 250g shortcrust pastry, 200g mixed fruit (fresh or canned), 30g sugar, 1 tablespoon cornflour, 1 egg (for egg wash)

US: 9oz shortcrust pastry, 1 cup mixed fruit (fresh or canned), ¼ cup sugar, 1 tablespoon cornstarch, 1 egg (for egg wash)

Instructions:

1. Preheat your air fryer to 200°C (400°F).
2. Roll out the pastry and cut it into circles for the mini pies.
3. In a bowl, mix the fruit with sugar and corn flour.
4. Spoon the fruit mixture onto half of the pastry circles and fold over. Seal the edges with a fork.
5. Brush with beaten egg before placing it in the air fryer.
6. Bake for 10-12 minutes until golden brown. Allow to cool slightly before serving!

Nutritional Info: Calories: 220 | Fat: 9g | Carbs: 34g | Protein: 2g

MEAL PLANNING AND NUTRITION GUIDE

60-DAY MEAL PLAN

Let's sort out a 60-day worth of delicious, nutritionally balanced vegetarian meals. I've designed this plan to be flexible, practical, and most importantly, absolutely scrummy, categorised by weeks and divided into breakfast, lunch, appetizer, dinner, and a special occasion Sunday dinner:

WEEK 1

DAYS	BREAKFAST	LUNCH	Appetizer	DINNER
MONDAY	Sweet Potato Toast Two Ways	Stuffed Bell Peppers	Crispy Cauliflower Wings	Eggplant Parmesan
TUESDAY	Apple-Cinnamon Oatmeal Cups	Tofu Fish and Chips	Appetizer: Mozzarella Sticks	Chickpea and Spinach Patties
WEDNESDAY	French Toast Sticks	Vegetable Lasagna Roll-Ups	Spinach and Artichoke Rolls	Mushroom Wellington
THURSDAY	Granola Clusters	Mediterranean Stuffed Courgettes	Sweet Potato Crisps	Quinoa and Black Bean Patties
FRIDAY	Crispy Tofu Scramble	Stuffed Potato Skins	Onion Bhajis	Cauliflower Steak Burger
SATURDAY	Cornmeal Pancake Bites	Lentil and Vegetable Loaf	Vegetable Spring Rolls	Crispy Tempeh Buddha Bowl
SUNDAY (SPECIAL DINNER)	Breakfast Quesadillas	Roasted Red Pepper Hummus (with veggie dippers)	Stuffed Jalapeño Poppers	Mushroom Wellington with Herb-Roasted Root Vegetables

WEEK 2

DAYS	BREAKFAST	LUNCH	Appetizer	DINNER
MONDAY	Crispy Hash Brown Nests with Avocado	Mediterranean Roasted Vegetables	Zucchini Chips	Tofu Fish and Chips
TUESDAY	Cinnamon Roll Bites	Roasted Cherry Tomatoes	Buffalo Cauliflower Bites	Stuffed Bell Peppers
WEDNESDAY	Breakfast Burrito Roll-Ups	Eggplant Parmesan	Crispy Okra Fries	Quinoa and Black Bean Patties
THURSDAY	Granola Clusters	Vegetable Antipasto Platter	Stuffed Mushroom Caps	Crispy Tofu Katsu Curry
FRIDAY	Sweet Potato Toast Two Ways	Cauliflower Rice	Crispy Chickpeas Three Ways	Vegetable Lasagna Roll-Ups
SATURDAY	Apple-Cinnamon Oatmeal Cups	Mediterranean Stuffed Courgettes	Crispy Mushroom "Calamari"	Mushroom Wellington
SUNDAY (SPECIAL DINNER)	French Toast Sticks	Cashew Cheese Sauce (with roasted veggies)	Corn Riblets	Lentil and Vegetable Loaf with Crispy Onion Strings

WEEK 3

DAYS	BREAKFAST	LUNCH	Appetizer	DINNER
MONDAY	Crispy Hash Brown Nests with Avocado	Chickpea and Spinach Patties	Mozzarella Sticks	Stuffed Potato Skins
TUESDAY	Cornmeal Pancake Bites	Crispy Polenta Chips	Zucchini Chips	Mushroom Wellington
WEDNESDAY	Breakfast Quesadillas	Crispy Tofu Katsu Curry	Onion Bhajis	Vegetable Lasagna Roll-Ups
THURSDAY	Apple-Cinnamon Oatmeal Cups	Stuffed Baby Potatoes	Buffalo Cauliflower Bites	Tofu Fish and Chips
FRIDAY	French Toast Sticks	Stuffed Bell Peppers	Crispy Mushroom "Calamari"	Crispy Tempeh Buddha Bowl
SATURDAY	Granola Clusters	Eggplant Parmesan	Vegetable Spring Rolls	Cauliflower Steak Burger
SUNDAY (SPECIAL DINNER)	Sweet Potato Toast Two Ways	Baba Ganoush (with pitta and veggies)	Spinach and Artichoke Rolls	Eggplant Parmesan with Mediterranean Aubergine Rounds

WEEK 4

DAYS	BREAKFAST	LUNCH	Appetizer	DINNER
MONDAY	Crispy Tofu Scramble	Quinoa and Black Bean Patties	Stuffed Jalapeño Poppers	Chickpea and Spinach Patties
TUESDAY	Breakfast Burrito Roll-Ups	Cauliflower Steaks	Sweet Potato Crisps	Lentil and Vegetable Loaf
WEDNESDAY	Cinnamon Roll Bites	Mediterranean Roasted Vegetables	Zucchini Chips	Tofu Fish and Chips
THURSDAY	French Toast Sticks	Stuffed Bell Peppers	Crispy Okra Fries	Mushroom Wellington
FRIDAY	Granola Clusters	Crispy Quinoa	Vegetable Spring Rolls	Vegetable Lasagna Roll-Ups
SATURDAY	Sweet Potato Toast Two Ways	Stuffed Potato Skins	Buffalo Cauliflower Bites	Mushroom Wellington
SUNDAY (SPECIAL DINNER)	Apple-Cinnamon Oatmeal Cups	Roasted Vegetable Pesto (with pasta)	Onion Bhajis	Cauliflower Steak Burger with Herbed Dinner Rolls

WEEK 5

DAYS	BREAKFAST	LUNCH	Appetizer	DINNER
MONDAY	Breakfast Quesadillas	Crispy Tempeh Buddha Bowl	Spinach and Artichoke Rolls	Quinoa and Black Bean Patties
TUESDAY	Sweet Potato Toast Two Ways	Tofu Fish and Chips	Crispy Chickpeas Three Ways	Chickpea and Spinach Patties
WEDNESDAY	Cornmeal Pancake Bites	Cauliflower Steak Burger	Onion Bhajis	Vegetable Lasagna Roll-Ups
THURSDAY	Granola Clusters	Mediterranean Roasted Vegetables	Buffalo Cauliflower Bites	Mushroom Wellington
FRIDAY	Cinnamon Roll Bites	Stuffed Bell Peppers	Zucchini Chips	Stuffed Potato Skins
SATURDAY	Crispy Hash Brown Nests with Avocado	Lentil and Vegetable Loaf	Mozzarella Sticks	Crispy Tofu Katsu Curry
SUNDAY (SPECIAL DINNER)	French Toast Sticks	Smoky Vegan Queso (with tortilla chips)	Sweet Potato Crisps	Tofu Fish and Chips with Garlic Herb Roasted Potatoes

WEEK 6

DAYS	BREAKFAST	LUNCH	Appetizer	DINNER
MONDAY	Sweet Potato Toast Two Ways	Vegetable Lasagna Roll-Ups	Stuffed Jalapeño Poppers	Cauliflower Steak Burger
TUESDAY	Granola Clusters	Stuffed Bell Peppers	Vegetable Spring Rolls	Mushroom Wellington
WEDNESDAY	Apple-Cinnamon Oatmeal Cups	Chickpea and Spinach Patties	Crispy Mushroom "Calamari"	Quinoa and Black Bean Patties
THURSDAY	Cornmeal Pancake Bites	Mediterranean Stuffed Courgettes	Onion Bhajis	Crispy Tempeh Buddha Bowl
FRIDAY	Breakfast Quesadillas	Tofu Fish and Chips	Zucchini Chips	Stuffed Potato Skins
SATURDAY	French Toast Sticks	Lentil and Vegetable Loaf	Buffalo Cauliflower Bites	Vegetable Lasagna Roll-Ups
SUNDAY (SPECIAL DINNER)	Cinnamon Roll Bites	Roasted Tomato Salsa (with tortilla chips)	Spinach and Artichoke Rolls	Eggplant Parmesan with Herb-Roasted Root Vegetables

WEEK 7

DAYS	BREAKFAST	LUNCH	Appetizer	DINNER
MONDAY	Sweet Potato Toast Two Ways	Stuffed Baby Potatoes	Crispy Chickpeas Three Ways	Mushroom Wellington
TUESDAY	Crispy Hash Brown Nests with Avocado	Mediterranean Roasted Vegetables	Mozzarella Sticks	Cauliflower Steak Burger
WEDNESDAY	Apple-Cinnamon Oatmeal Cups	Quinoa and Black Bean Patties	Vegetable Spring Rolls	Crispy Tempeh Buddha Bowl
THURSDAY	Breakfast Burrito Roll-Ups	Crispy Tofu Katsu Curry	Sweet Potato Crisps	Vegetable Lasagna Roll-Ups
FRIDAY	Cornmeal Pancake Bites	Stuffed Potato Skins	Onion Bhajis	Tofu Fish and Chips
SATURDAY	Granola Clusters	Stuffed Bell Peppers	Crispy Mushroom "Calamari	Chickpea and Spinach Patties
SUNDAY (SPECIAL DINNER)	Cinnamon Roll Bites	Romesco Sauce (with roasted vegetables)	Buffalo Cauliflower Bites	Lentil and Vegetable Loaf with Mediterranean Aubergine Rounds

WEEK 8

DAYS	BREAKFAST	LUNCH	Appetizer	DINNER
MONDAY	Sweet Potato Toast Two Ways	Eggplant Parmesan	Spinach and Artichoke Rolls	Cauliflower Steak Burger
TUESDAY	Apple-Cinnamon Oatmeal Cups	Tofu Fish and Chips	Zucchini Chips	Mushroom Wellington
WEDNESDAY	French Toast Sticks	Quinoa and Black Bean Patties	Crispy Chickpeas Three Ways	Stuffed Bell Peppers
THURSDAY	Cornmeal Pancake Bites	Crispy Tempeh Buddha Bowl	Mozzarella Sticks	Vegetable Lasagna Roll-Ups
FRIDAY	Granola Clusters	Stuffed Potato Skins	Sweet Potato Crisps	Crispy Tofu Katsu Curry
SATURDAY	Crispy Tofu Scramble	Mediterranean Stuffed Courgettes	Onion Bhajis	Mushroom Wellington
SUNDAY (SPECIAL DINNER)	Breakfast Quesadillas	Roasted Red Pepper Hummus (with veggie sticks)	Corn Riblets	Quinoa and Black Bean Patties with Herbed Dinner Rolls

WEEK 9

DAYS	BREAKFAST	LUNCH	Appetizer	DINNER
MONDAY	Sweet Potato Toast Two Ways	Chickpea and Spinach Patties	Stuffed Jalapeño Poppers	Cauliflower Steak Burger
TUESDAY	Granola Clusters	Lentil and Vegetable Loaf	Crispy Okra Fries	Mushroom Wellington
WEDNESDAY	Cinnamon Roll Bites	Quinoa and Black Bean Patties	Spinach and Artichoke Rolls	Tofu Fish and Chips
THURSDAY	Apple-Cinnamon Oatmeal Cups	Stuffed Baby Potatoes	Crispy Mushroom "Calamari"	Crispy Tofu Katsu Curry

PREP AHEAD SUNDAY:

Make granola (keeps all week)
Prep vegetables for Monday and Tuesday
Cook extra chickpeas for Wednesday's burgers

SHOPPING LISTS

Week 1 Shopping List

Produce
2 aubergines
1 butternut squash
500g mushrooms
[Continued list]

Proteins
2 blocks of firm tofu
400g tempeh
[Continued list]

Pantry
Chickpeas (2 tins)
Brown rice
[Continued list]

Herbs & Spices
Fresh coriander
Cumin
[Continued list]

Money-saving Tips
1. Buy seasonal veg
2. Check frozen options
3. Batch cook and freeze
4. Use dried legumes instead of tinned

PREP AHEAD TIPS

Weekend Prep (2 hours)

1. Hour 1:
  Wash and chop all veg
  Prepare marinades
  Soak legumes

2. Hour 2:
  Cook grains
  Make sauces
  Prepare protein (press tofu, etc.)

Weeknight Timesavers

1. 10Minute Morning Prep
  Take items from the freezer
  Marinate proteins
  Quick veg prep

2. Post Work Efficiency
  Air fryer preheating routine
  3step meal assembly

CONVERSIONS AND SUBSTITUTIONS

MEASUREMENT CONVERSIONS

VOLUME CONVERSIONS

UK	US	Metric
1 tablespoon	1 tablespoon	15ml
1 teaspoon	1 teaspoon	5ml
1 cup	1.2 cups	250ml

WEIGHT CONVERSIONS

UK	US	Metric
1 pound	1 pound	454g
1 ounce	1 ounce	28g
1 stone	14 pounds	6.35kg

COMMON SUBSTITUTIONS

Egg Replacements (for binding)

1 egg = 1 tablespoon ground flaxseed + 3 tablespoons water
1 egg = 60g mashed banana
1 egg = 60ml aquafaba

PROTEIN SUBSTITUTIONS

Instead Of	Try This	Cooking Adjustment

Chicken	Cauliflower	Increase temp by 10°C
Fish	Marinated tofu	Reduce cooking time by 2 mins
Minced meat	Lentil & walnut mix	Add more moisture

ADAPTING REGULAR RECIPES FOR AIR FRYER

General Rules

1. Temperature
Reduce by 20°C
Check 5 minutes earlier

2. Oil Usage
Reduce to 1 tablespoon max

Use a spray for even coating

3. Size Matters
Cut items smaller
Don't overcrowd the basket

COMMON ADAPTATIONS

Original Method	Air Fryer Method	Tips
Deep frying	Air fry at 200°C	Spray with oil
Roasting	Air fry at 180°C	Shake basket often
Baking	Air fry at 160°C	Use parchment paper

CONVERSION CHART

Oven Temperature	Air Fryer Temperature	Time Adjustment
220°C	200°C	Reduce by 20%
200°C	180°C	Reduce by 15%
180°C	160°C	Reduce by 10%

Remember: These guidelines are just starting points. Every air fryer is different, so don't be afraid to experiment and find what works best for your specific model. Keep notes, trust your instincts, and most importantly, enjoy the journey to becoming an air fryer veggie expert!

Printed in Great Britain
by Amazon